"Maryann N. Weidt makes wonderfully readable the career and works of the pivotal writer who has made contact with the young at just that point when their parents fail to. The chapter on the censorship from right and left visited upon Judy Blume is alone worth the price of this book."

—Richard Peck

Maryann N. Weidt is the former head of Children's and Young Adult Services at the Duluth Public Library.

ALSO AVAILABLE IN LAUREL-LEAF BOOKS:

PRESENTING
JUDY BLUME

MARYANN N. WEIDT

Published by
Dell Publishing
a division of
Bantam Doubleday Dell Publishing Group, Inc.
666 Fifth Avenue
New York, New York 10103

Photographs kindly provided by Judy Blume.
Cover photo by George Cooper.

ISBN: 0-440-21093-3

RL: 9.4

Reprinted by arrangement with G. K. Hall & Co., on behalf of Twayne Publishers

Printed in the United States of America

October 1991

10 9 8 7 6 5 4 3 2 1

RAD

To David
He always made me laugh

Contents

Preface

Crossing the Street in New York City

I walk up Broadway, past Lincoln Center, following the route she has given me. It is winter and the day has turned warm, yet I am clad in the dark wool coat, knee socks, and short lined boots I brought with me from Minnesota. It is a few minutes before one o'clock. My throat is raw. I suck a cough drop.

I turn at the street indicated in the directions. When I come to the corner, I wait for the light to turn green. It does and I step off the curb. A thick, chocolate-colored Mercedes is backing toward me. I see it out of the corner of my eye. I hear a New York City voice yell an obscenity. From deep inside my raspy throat come the words, "Hey, watch it, buddy!" I cross the street, feeling proud of my rapid adjustment to my new surroundings. I pass shops selling fancy cookware, designer clothes, and what Minnesotans call gourmet food. New Yorkers call it deli. I begin to check the numbers on the buildings. I approach the intersection with caution, looking both ways, even though it is a one-way street. Watch for cars backing up, I remind myself. There are no vehicles approaching from either direction. I begin to cross. Halfway across the street, I glance up at the light. It's flaming red. I am crossing a street in New York City against a red light. Madness has overcome me. The throat lozenges have affected my judgment. Quickly, I check left and right and continue hastily across. Standing safely on the sidewalk, I inhale deeply and consult my watch. It is one minute to one.

My feet are like cement in my sturdy boots, but I run the last half block to the building with the number I am seeking. Up three steps. Open the door. Walk in. A doorman approaches. Breathlessly, I tell him my name and utter the words I do not believe. "I'm here to see Judy Blume." Exhale.

I ride the elevator to the sixteenth floor. The penthouse. She opens the door. The smile is an ad for her late father's profession. In dark trousers and delicate pale peach cashmere sweater, she looks fragile, though I know she is not. I am enormous in my great wool coat and heavy boots, which she invites me to leave in a downstairs anteroom. "Have you had lunch?" she asks encouragingly. "Only throat discs," I confess. She leads me to the skylit kitchen, where she opens the refrigerator. "I think I have some leftovers from the Society of Children's Book Writers meeting." She brings out cheese and apples and lays them on the solid butcher block countertop.

I am afraid to look around. A hard gaze could send the entire scene back inside Aladdin's lamp. I am afraid to move. A false step will surely send me hurtling backward against a wall of southwestern Indian pottery. I prop myself against a kitchen counter and lean there.

We talk about our children as she slices mold from the chunk of orange cheese. "You don't mind, do you?" she asks innocently. "It's good cheese. It's from Zabar's" (*the* local deli). I assure her I am quite in the habit of eating moldy cheese, if the children don't get to it first. Thank God for the children. We are mothers talking about our children. And two of mine are adopted, as is one of the characters in the book she's currently finishing. She sighs wistfully and wonders aloud if she shouldn't have adopted a child. The past seven years have been the happiest she has ever known. The relationship has a feeling of permanency to it. She may just grow old with this man who makes her laugh. They practice together saying fifty, referring to their impending ages. "George will have to say it before I do," Blume teases. By now we have finished our munching of cheese, crackers, and apples, and her husband, George Cooper, has come in from his daily run to join us for Walker shortbread cookies and coffee. Blume has made coffee using a plunger-type coffee maker, a copy of which I vow I will purchase at the fancy cookware shop en route back to my hotel.

We move with coffee cups and cookies to the white and wicker of the living room. Is this my cue to begin the serious questioning? I hit the record button and say a silent prayer to the god of all mechanical things. I begin, "In *Tiger Eyes* Davey, the main character says, *'La vida es una buena aventura,* Life is a great adventure.' Do you consider yourself an adventurous person?" Cooper, sensing the story that is approaching, excuses himself, while Blume good-naturedly taunts him that it is no excuse to say he's heard it all before, even though he has. We all laugh, and as Cooper retreats, Blume launches into an account of a trip she and George made through the Florida Everglades several years ago. She paints a picture of herself paddling through the swamp and slogging through muck wearing knee-high dress boots ("I threw them out when we got home") and khaki shorts. "I knew the snakes couldn't bite through those boots," she announces proudly. *"That* was an adventure! . . . Then there was the time George and I took four teenagers on a sailboat from Seattle along the coast of British Columbia and back for five weeks. We were supposed to catch fish but we didn't and there wasn't much wind for sailing. So we putted around and ate macaroni and cheese, canned tuna, and spaghetti. That was *definitely* an adventure."

I am beginning to think she might appreciate my tale of near-death at a New York City intersection when she smiles in the direction Cooper has departed and says, warmly, "George teases that for me a great adventure is crossing the street in New York City *with* the light."

I smile. I want to hug her. I know I am going to like this woman.

Thank you, Judy Blume, for allowing me to share a part of your life in New York City for two unbelievable days in December of 1986. You made my job wonderfully easy. It was like talking to an old friend. Thank you, George Cooper, for your good-natured tolerance of the intrusion. Larry Blume, thank you for taking time away from your filmmaking to tell me about yourself and your mother. Thank you, Richard Jackson, for taking time from your editing to give me your perspective on Judy Blume's career. A carload of wild rice would not be enough to thank all of you for what you have done for me.

Quotations throughout the book not attributable to any other source are from tape-recorded notes of my conversations with Judy Blume, Larry Blume, and Richard Jackson on 15 and 16 December 1986 in New York City.

Barbara Rollock, former Children's Services Coordinator with the New York Public Library, was kind enough to meet with me while I was in New York City. Quotations from Ms. Rollock that appear in the text without other documentation are from a tape-recorded interview on 17 December 1986.

I also wish to thank the entire staff of the Duluth Public Library for their research assistance and moral support. I am indebted to Kären Richgruber and Judy Sheriff and the complete Children's Area crew for their tolerance and support during the project.

Thank you to my writers' group: Julie Ball, who instilled in me the importance of an outline; Ann Schimpf, who read and corrected my sample chapter; and Fran Weber, who helped me learn to love my computer.

Thank you to Judy Delton, Cynthia Driscoll, Gary Paulsen, and Jane Resh Thomas for encouraging words aptly placed.

Thank you for responding to my calls for help: Frank Bataglia, Ken Donelson, Carol Erdahl, Leanne Katz,

Norma Klein, John Korty, Ginny Moore Kruse, Gabrielle Lange, Kaye McKinzie, Mary Morse, Allen Raymond, Claire Smith, Molly Stein, and Sue Yunis.

Thank you to Virginia Duncan at Bradbury Press and Mimi Kayden at Dutton for providing me with copies of Blume books for children and young adults.

Thank you to Athenaide Dallett for guidance throughout the project and an enormous thank you to Patty Campbell, who showed me, among other things, the value of a topic sentence.

Finally, to all friends, neighbors, and library users who asked repeatedly, "Isn't that book out yet?"—thank you for your concern. Here it is.

Maryann N. Weidt

Duluth, Minnesota

Chronology

1938 Judy Sussman born 12 February in Elizabeth, New Jersey.

1959 July, Rudolph Sussman (father) dies. 15 August, marries John M. Blume.

1960 Receives B.A. in education, New York University.

1961 22 February, Randy Lee (daughter) born.

1963 5 July, Lawrence Andrew (Larry) born.

1966 Begins writing stories for children.

1969 *The One in the Middle Is the Green Kangaroo.*

1970 *Iggie's House. Are You There God? It's Me, Margaret.*

1971 *Freckle Juice. Then Again, Maybe I Won't.*

1972 *It's Not the End of the World. Tales of a Fourth Grade Nothing. Otherwise Known as Sheila the Great.*

1973 *Deenie.*

1974 *Blubber.*

1975 *Forever.* Divorces Blume, moves to Princeton, New Jersey.

1976 8 May, marries Thomas A. Kitchens, moves to New Mexico.

1977 *Starring Sally J. Freedman as Herself.*

1978 *Wifey.*

1979 Divorces Kitchens.

1980 *Superfudge.*

1981 *Tiger Eyes.* KIDS Fund established. *The Judy Blume Diary.*

1983 *Smart Women.*

1984 *The Pain and the Great One.*

1985 Moves to New York City.

1986 *Letters to Judy: What Your Kids Wish They Could Tell You.*

1987 6 June, marries George Cooper. Esther Sussman (mother) dies. *Just As Long As We're Together.*

1988 Writes and produces film of *Otherwise Known as Sheila the Great. The Judy Blume Memory Book.*

1990 *Fudge-a-mania.*

1

Starring Judy Sussman

Judy Blume began her adventure as a writer of children's books with an invitation from publisher Richard Jackson to visit him at Bradbury Press to discuss a manuscript she had submitted. Blume recalls the day with vivid trepidation. "My stomach was rolling, so I took something to calm it, but whatever I took dried up my mouth so that I could barely speak." Mr. Jackson remembers that they went to lunch and that Blume ate nothing. Blume denies there was a luncheon in connection with that first meeting. She says, "I remember thinking, 'Will he invite me for lunch?' and he didn't. Dick and his partner ordered sandwiches, and I left."

With or without lunch, Richard Jackson became Judy Blume's editor and lifelong friend. Jackson, when asked if he saw stardom for Blume in that first manuscript, says, "I saw not just that manuscript [which was *Iggie's House*], but I saw the next book and the next book and the next. Actually, my partner, Bob Verrone had handed it to me and said, 'You should read this.' What was immediately obvious was that she had an incredible ear for dialogue." *Iggie's House* is a book that Blume now wishes she could rewrite or throw out. "And yet, I can't believe it," she says. "There are kids that will come up to me and say, '*Iggie's House* is my favorite book.' I guess there must be something there that they identify with."

As every aspiring writer does, Blume sent stories to magazines and manuscripts to publishers, and like millions of mothers of young children, she read stories to her two toddlers every night before they went to bed. When she ran out of books from the library, she made up stories while she washed the dinner dishes. Before long she was sending these stories, along with her own illustrations ("I can't draw a stick," she admits now) to all the major publishers.

One day in the mail arrived, along with several rejection notices, a flyer advertising an evening class in writing for children at New York University, her alma mater. Blume knew this was an omen. Why would she have received the brochure if she wasn't supposed to take the class? Her father had told her the world was full of adventure. This would be an adventure. She took the class—not once, but twice. She was working on *Iggie's House,* and every week she turned in a chapter. "That way I felt I was getting my money's worth," she laughs. The instructor was encouraging. Her advice: "Stick to your realistic fiction. It's what you do best." "I don't think I knew that," Blume comments.

While she was enrolled in the class at NYU, Blume sold her first story to a children's magazine. The story was called "The Ooh Ooh Aah Aah Bird." The magazine paid Blume twenty dollars for it, and her writing instructor brought her a red rose.

Another early story that Blume remembers writing was based on her son, Larry, and his relationship with ladybugs. "When he was very young, he would sit in the backyard and collect ladybugs and talk to them," she recalls.

One of Blume's early efforts was never published as a story but later grew into a chapter in *Tales of a Fourth Grade Nothing.* The story was originally called "Roger Crater" or "Mrs. Crater's Worries." It was about a child who did not want to eat. "This was not based on my own children," she says, "because they always enjoyed their food. However, my brother and I, I am told, did not like to eat."

When the class at NYU ended, *Iggie's House* was finished. But where to send it? Blume saw an ad in a writer's magazine ("I used to subscribe to all of them," she confesses) for a new publishing company that was interested in realistic fiction for eight- to twelve-year-olds. The publishing company, of course, was Bradbury Press. Richard Jackson recalls that the company, which was young and struggling at the time, spent "practically the only $5,000 we had" to run that ad. He says now, "It was the best $5,000 we ever spent."

After her first meeting with Dick Jackson, Blume went home and rewrote—and rewrote. Jackson says, "I never see a manuscript from Judy that she has not rewritten six or seven times. By the time I see it, she usually knows what, if anything, is wrong with it. Sometimes she simply needs me to tell her. We talk about the characters and she writes herself pages of notes."

Blume admits that she always knows more about her characters than she has written. Talking with Jackson about the characters is an important part of the writing process for her. As Jackson puts it, "We do a lot of talking. I do a lot of talking and she does a lot of talking and ultimately the characters do a lot of their talking."

When there are changes that need to be made in a manuscript, Blume does not hesitate to make them. In *Margaret,* for example, Jackson felt an additional scene dealing with one of the grandmothers needed to be added. Blume agreed and added it. In *Just As Long As We're Together* she created an entirely new beginning in order to establish the relationship between two of the girls and cut thirty pages out of another section that she and Jackson felt was too long and wordy.

Jackson says, "She is an absolute professional in that she is not vain about her work, but she is committed to the integrity of the work in question. No amount of work is too great in order for the writing to say what she means it to say. She will whittle and fiddle and polish and tinker in ways that would astonish people."

Most of Blume's whittling and polishing is done in an office in her New York apartment overlooking the Hudson River. She no longer shares a work space with her husband, who is also a writer. She says, "When I am working in the same room with someone, I am easily distracted. If the phone rings, I listen in on half of the conversation. Thus, George and I have separated, at least when we are working."

For years, Blume preferred the feel of an electric typewriter. Cooper, who uses the latest in word processing equipment, has persuaded her to try a computer. "I wrote *Fudge-a-mania* on the computer," she says proudly.

When Blume completed the rewrite on *Iggie's House,* she and Jackson met again, and this time there was a contract to sign—and lunch. "I don't know if I ate anything," Blume says, "but I do remember making a silly joke to the waiter about his having dropped something in my water glass. It was a lemon slice. He was very pompous, and he replied, 'Madam, I drop that in everyone's glass.'"

Iggie's House, however, was not destined to be Judy Blume's first book, although it was the first book that mattered, as it began her lifelong relationship with Dick Jackson and Bradbury Press. While she was waiting to hear from Jackson, another small publisher, Reilly & Lee, called and offered her a contract on a picture book she had sent them entitled *The One in the Middle Is the Green Kangaroo.* Blume will never forget the day: "The children, then about five and seven years old, were in the basement playing with something called Silly Sand. It was like dried pieces of balsa wood. You soaked it in water and then you could mold it. It was very messy stuff. When they called to offer me the contract, I was so excited, I ran down the stairs and put my hands into this bowl of Silly Sand and threw it all over the place. Then I picked up the kids and spun them around. Laurie Murphy, Larry's best friend, looked at me and left, crying. She went home and told her mother that Larry's mother had gone crazy."

Judy Blume was an island in the suburban New Jersey setting in which she lived. She was twenty-seven years old. No other women she knew worked outside the home, and yet she had a burning desire to do something. She had a degree in education but did not want to teach because she preferred being at home with her children. She began making felt pictures, some of which she sold on consignment to Bloomingdale's. "One of my friends still has one," Blume says. "She thinks it's a collector's item."

When Blume began to think of writing as a career, there was little if any support from friends or neighbors. "I don't think any of us at that time ever really admitted what we were feeling or what life was like or what our hopes and dreams were," she recalls. She describes suburban New Jersey of the sixties as "the most deadly, apathetic, noninvolved place on earth."

"When I started to write, there were a lot of people who were genuinely resentful. The lack of support was jarring," Blume admits. Yet there was one neighbor, a woman who later became a librarian, who shared Blume's joy and pride when reviews of her books appeared in the *New York Times.*

Blume's husband, John Blume, did not discourage his wife from writing, but he did not encourage her either. "He thought it was better than shopping," Blume says, which was a favorite pastime of other suburban wives. "Those women weren't even shopping," she continues, "but simply going to the stores, for lack of anything better to do."

As Mrs. John M. Blume, her job was to run the house, raise the children, and make life easy for her husband. "This was what suburban women did in the sixties," Blume says. She took tennis lessons and golf lessons, so that she could hold up her end on a court or a course. But Blume, who prides herself on excelling in anything she attempts, was a failure on the fairway. "I would do fine during the lesson, but as soon as I got to the game, I would freeze. I think it had something to do with someone telling me, 'You must do this.' I'm still like that. Tell me I have to do something and I dig in my heels in refusal."

Blume's illnesses were also a substantial part of her life at this time. She recommends reading *Wifey* for a better understanding of her various exotic diseases. "The minute my first book was published," she says, "I never had another serious illness."

Judy Sussman had become Mrs. John M. Blume on 15 August 1959, following her junior year at New York University. Sadly, the wedding took place only five weeks after the death of Judy's father, her beloved Doey-bird. Since the date of a Jewish wedding, once set, cannot be changed, the ceremony took place as planned. Blume says, "It was not a weepy wedding. My father was such a jolly, loving, philosophical person, and everyone knew that he would insist that it go on and that we smile. And we did."

Blume was emotionally overwhelmed by her father's death, perhaps more so than she ever realized at the time. She had experienced death in her childhood: a cousin, three grandparents, and six aunts and uncles. Two of the uncles, who also were dentists, had died when they were forty-two years old. When Judy's father turned forty-two, she was terrified. She made endless deals with God to keep him alive and became extremely ritualistic. Reflecting on it now, Blume says, "That was a tremendous responsibility for a child."

Judy's father was forty-two the year the family lived in Miami, and Judy was, for the most part, separated from him. The family moved to Florida for the sake of her brother David's health. He suffered from a kidney infection and the doctors told the Sussmans that a warm climate would be beneficial. Because of Dr. Sussman's dental practice, he was able to join the family only every few weeks. Judy grew up a lot that year. She learned to be independent of her father, although she wrote him countless letters. It was also the year she began to see her father as a separate person, with his own dreams and desires.

Blume remembers that when she was a young teenager her father told her that the family might move to Nevada. She would have horses. It would be a genuine wild west adventure. But reality stepped in, and that dream never came true. "My father was an extremely adventurous person," Blume says, "who didn't get to live out his adventures. He loved the idea of change and adventure. I wanted to be like my father, but in my early years I was certainly like my mother."

Blume's mother wanted absolutely no changes in her life. Blume says, "Her schedule was so exact that I knew every night when she was cooking and what she was cooking. Changes were frightening to her." When Judy's father died, however, Mrs. Sussman was forced to make some changes in her life. Her sister convinced her to go back to work—she had been a legal secretary before her marriage—and she worked for about ten years before retiring.

Mrs. Sussman died of pneumonia in the summer of 1987 with her daughter at her side. During the last week of her mother's life, Blume sat with her day and night. "I will always be grateful for that one week in the hospital," Blume says. "I was able to say good-bye, and we got to tell each other that we loved one another." Blume tried for years to unravel her relationship with her mother. Before her mother's death, she said, "I would like, now especially, to understand her." But given their opposite personalities—Mrs. Sussman, who "was not an easy talker," and "kept everything inside," and Blume, who talks freely and keeps little inside—it was a monumental task. Blume is thankful that her mother enjoyed a long life (she was eighty-three when she died) and that she was able to maintain her independence, which, Blume says, she "valued above all else." She recalls that the week before she was hospitalized, her mother had driven to a nearby shopping mall, had lunch with a friend and bought herself a white bag, on sale, for the next summer.

Blume is also thankful that she and George were married while her mother was alive. She recalls, "She always said, 'I should only live to see this wedding.' And she did." The ceremony took place on 6 June 1987 on the balcony of the couple's New York apartment. A judge, who is a friend of Blume and Cooper, read a poem about loving and growing as part of the ritual. Blume says, "Since she knew both of us she was able to make the brief ceremony very personal." The couple honeymooned in New Hampshire, where Blume spoke to eight hundred youngsters. "I loved sharing my honeymoon with them!" she says. "And they loved it too."

Although Blume is happy now, pain and disappointment have played a part in her life. After sixteen years she saw her marriage to John Blume crumble. She talks openly and easily about her first marriage. "I don't think my choice of John was wrong at the time. It reflected everything I knew of life. I was twenty-one years old." Blume hopes that today's young people will make wiser, more informed choices but admits that she probably would not have listened to anyone at that age "because you can say to somebody, here's what's important, but when those chills hit and there's something going on. . . ."

After several detours, Blume has found that the road to a strong relationship is paved with humor. "George makes me laugh," she confides. "He is very funny, but he is only funny for me, he says." She elaborates on the importance of humor in any relationship. "It needs to be there, and it needs to be compatible. There is nothing better than waking up every morning and laughing about something and going to bed at night and laughing about something. What a wonderful way to live." Blume uses her sense of humor to cope with the intensely serious moments in her life. She says that "humor is often the only way to get through a difficult situation."[1]

Blume looks back on her divorce from her first husband as part of a rebellion that was going on inside her. She wanted adventure, perhaps the adventure her father promised was so much a part of life. She says that following her divorce, she "wanted to taste and experience *life*. I wasn't terrible. I was responsible. I was working. I loved the kids. But I was rebelling, I think, in ways one should rebel at seventeen. My divorce was all part of that rebellion."

Blume knows and readily admits that she has made mistakes with her children. She says she doesn't trust any parent who claims they haven't. "I can remember saying to my kids, 'You can blame me forever, or we can get on with it'— so we got on with it."

They may have gotten on with it, but Blume carried with her the guilt of moving her children from one location to another. She says, "They lived in one house until they were nine and eleven. And then I just dragged them all over the place." Blume sees a parent's decision to move as a symbol of the child's lack of control of their life. "What choices do kids have? . . . I look at my kids and I think how I've disrupted their lives so many times! We've all gotten through it somehow, but it certainly wasn't easy for them."[2] The theme of moving emerges repeatedly in Blume's writing.

Even before his parents' separation, Larry Blume, her younger child, had changed schools several times by the time he was in third grade. To add to his problems, he had very poor small motor skills. "He could smash a baseball over the house," Blume says, "but he couldn't hold a pencil." In fourth grade it was a different school again because the family had moved, and in fifth and sixth grades, it was a small private school.

When Larry was in sixth grade and Randy in eighth grade, Judy and John Blume separated, and Judy moved with the children to Princeton, New Jersey. Larry spent half of seventh grade in Princeton and half in London, where Blume had moved with Tom Kitchens, the physicist she later married. During the year in London, Larry was doing his own rebelling. "He was pretty horrible," Blume admits. "He acted out all his feelings about the divorce, while saying, 'I don't care if you're getting a divorce.' "

On returning from London, Blume married Kitchens, and she and the children moved to Los Alamos, New Mexico, a move that was painful for both Blume and her children. She recalls sadly, "Randy absolutely detested Los Alamos, almost from the moment she got there." Yet Randy was attracted by the mountains and became a mountain climber; at seventeen she was part of an Outward Bound summer expedition. Blume says of Los Alamos, "It is a town with very frustrated, resentful, talented women who have very few outlets and few job opportunities."

Blume, always interested in the education of her children, was concerned about the schools in Los Alamos. "It drove me crazy that in this community of brilliant scientists, the kids in school were not given the opportunity to think and were not rewarded for thinking." She tells of Randy submitting a poem written in lower case letters and being reprimanded for it. The teacher's comment was, "Who do you think you are, e.e. cummings?"

Besides her unhappiness with the town, Blume was miserable in her second marriage. "We didn't know each other," she admits. "I cried for four years, but I learned a lot." Blume feels that she never rebelled as an adolescent but sees herself from thirty-five to forty as a very late adolescent. She confesses, "It's not a time to be adolescent when your children are being adolescent."

Blume explains her "adolescent" choice of a second husband in these words: "I could have had affairs, but instead I got married because I thought that's what you did. So I married the first man who said, 'Hello, how are you?' He seemed like a very nice man, but I didn't know him at all and he didn't know me. And that was just disastrous."

Blume divorced Kitchens in 1979 but remained in New Mexico, in Santa Fe, until 1985. She had maintained an apartment in New York City since 1981. In her New York apartment she displays many artifacts—pottery and wall-hangings—of the Southwest. "I loved the white and the sunshine," she says. "I loved the bright colors."

Blume is close, both physically and emotionally, to her now grown-up children. She keeps in touch, usually by phone, with Larry, a filmmaker in New York City, and Randy, a former pilot for a major airline, at least weekly. Blume speaks lovingly of her relationship with her children: "With Larry," she says, "it's very easy. With Randy, I'm more careful. I think that's true of mothers and daughters, and I don't know that that's bad. We have a great deal of respect for each other."

Blume proudly acknowledges her daughter's recent literary endeavors. Randy, who is now married, is at work on a book about her experiences as a female pilot for a major airline. Blume boasts that what she has read of Randy's writing is "really quite good. It's warm and witty and funny."

Larry, who shares his mother's temperament, reveals this insight into her personality: "She's very open about her feelings. I'm the same way. I'll meet a stranger on the subway and tell them everything. Sometimes I'm too honest. It's easy to get hurt—especially in relationships." Both mother and son admit to being quick to anger on occasion but also quick to forgive. Blume explains, "I don't brood. I'm emotional and I might explode or throw things, or I might cry and carry on, but then it's over."

Blume may not give herself awards as a parent, but she is planning, given the opportunity, to be the best possible grandparent: the kind who shows up in most of her books, giving freely of her love, her time, and her sex education pamphlets. Blume's maternal grandmother was from the "old country," and she was very much loved by her children. She moved with the Sussmans to Florida and lived with them again when she became ill. She died of cancer when Judy was fifteen and away at summer camp. "She adored us and she'd never scold us. She sewed me beautiful doll clothes, and she cooked." Blume says, "I like to think that I would be a very involved grandmother, not pushy, but supportive and nonjudgmental of the children. Michelle's tap-dancing grandmother in *Smart Women:* that's me!"

Blume has given up tap dancing for now, explaining, "It was taking time away from my writing. In order to be good —and I like to be good at anything I do—I would have had to attend classes five or six days a week." When Judy Blume does something, she does it well.

When asked if there has been anything in her life at which

she has not excelled, she thinks immediately of precollege days and taking standardized college entrance exams. "When I went to take the SAT, I know now that what I had was some sort of anxiety attack. I looked at the page and it was all a blur. I made marks at random up and down the page." Since Judy had been an excellent student throughout high school, when her scores came back the guidance counselor called her in to find out what had happened. Judy refused to take the exam over again, stating flatly that she would apply only to colleges that would not place a high emphasis on the SAT score. She applied to Boston University, Syracuse, and an all-girl school in Pennsylvania called Cedarcrest. "I have no idea why I did that," she says laughing. "I was accepted at BU and Syracuse—and put on a waiting list at Cedarcrest."

Judy chose Boston University because it was a large school and because there were a lot of men there. She says candidly, "I went to college to be a teacher because I was influenced by my mother's practical wishes for me. I knew my goal in college was to meet a man and get married. My mother said to get a degree in education in case I ever *had* to work, but I wasn't really thinking. I was very busy wanting to get married and have babies and play grown-up."

Knowing that she wasn't feeling well and afraid to tell her parents for fear they would keep her home, Judy set out for Boston University in search of new adventures. After two weeks, she was too ill to attend classes. The school's doctor diagnosed her illness as mononucleosis. She was put on a plane and flown home on a stretcher. The ever-cautious Mrs. Sussman would not allow her daughter out of bed for several months. "The worst part," Blume remembers, "was that she wouldn't let me wash my hair or take a bath." As a mild rebellion, Judy let the hair on her legs grow and when her friends came to visit, she would stick out one leg to show them how long she had been without a bath.

To eighteen-year-old Judy Sussman, having to abandon her freshman year in college seemed like the end of the world. Blume wonders if she may not have become somewhat of a hypochondriac after her bout with mono. "I think I got a little crazy," she acknowledges. "I was afraid to go very far from home. When I went back to school, I went to New York University because it was only a car ride away."

Her ordeal with mono was not Judy's first encounter with disease. Her childhood illnesses were near legend among her family. Her daughter, Randy, says, "Mother, you were rewarded for getting sick." Blume concurs. "At least once a winter I could count on staying home from school, staying in bed, and listening to my 'stories' on the radio." Some of Judy's most creative moments as a child were spent sick in bed, playing paper dolls on the wooden bed table her father made for her.

Perhaps from listening to "stories" and going to movies with her mother every week, Judy developed a love of theatrics. "I wanted to be a movie star when I was young," she says. "Actually, I wanted to be Esther Williams, or at least her younger sister." Judy was involved in plays in high school, but she never was the star. In tenth grade she was part of the apprentice group of a modern dance ensemble, and by twelfth grade she had worked her way into the performing group. While Judy lived in Florida when she was nine, she made her debut as producer, director, and star by organizing a dance program to raise money for a Jewish charity organization with which her mother and grandmother were involved. Blume recalls, "We made costumes, and we even had programs. The programs read: 'Starring Judy Sussman, with . . . and . . .' because I knew that's how they did it in the movies."

When Judy returned to New Jersey from Florida, she directed a classroom production that she titled, "Stop the Music." Judy explains, "It was from a radio show, and they'd yell 'Stop the Music.' My show had at least five or six acts, complete with costumes." Judy's father put his creative talents to work and Judy became the Old Gold dancing cigarette box. She laughs, "Of course, we would never think of letting our children be cigarette boxes today." Blume has never smoked.

As a very young child Judy was neither a producer nor a director. She was extremely timid, probably because her mother was a shy person. She remembers hiding behind her mother's leg when a neighbor came to invite Judy to play with her little girl. "Rozzie's mother would come to our house and say, 'Let her come to our house; I'll make her spaghetti,' and my mother would say, 'She doesn't eat spaghetti.' " Blume finds this interesting, since she now consumes pasta on a regular basis.

Although Judy overcame her shyness, her brother David was an introvert and a loner throughout childhood. He had a workshop in the basement, and like Sally's brother in *Starring Sally J. Freedman as Herself* he actually sunburned the back of his neck under the workbench lamp. David was too busy with his scientific projects to worry about anything else. He was not a model student. Blume states it bluntly and somewhat angrily: "My brother did not please, and so I was the child who had to please. I think it's bad when you're a kid and you feel that your role in life is to please your parents and so the only news you come home with is happy news. I never felt that I could be sad or disappointed or even angry. I had to be Little Miss Sunshine all the time. That was my role in the family." She feels that that behavior has carried over into her adult life and that she still tries very hard to please people.

Judy Blume, at this point in her life, enjoys being an adult but feels a person never quite finishes growing up. "I'm constantly learning," she says. Blume's latest challenge actually involved being a producer. She and her son Larry worked together—she as producer, he as director—on the film version of *Otherwise Known as Sheila the Great*. For Blume there will always be a new challenge, a new adventure, a new street to cross.

2

Two Thousand
Letters a Month

Judy Blume is indisputably the most popular author of books for young people today. Indeed, Blume's books sell so fast that publishers and publicists alike have trouble keeping track of the number of volumes sold.

In August of 1982 *Time* magazine stated that "nineteen million of Blume's 14 teen tales are currently in paperback."[1] By December of 1983 Faith McNulty wrote in the *New Yorker:* "The hard cover sales of all her titles total more than a million, but the true measure of her audience is indicated by her paperback sales, which have been estimated at twenty-seven million."[2] Claire Smith, Blume's agent, suggests that a fairly accurate recent figure might be the one quoted on the cover of *Letters to Judy* in 1987: "35 million copies of her paperback books in print." Smith adds, "I can only assume that the figure has grown since then."[3] Indeed it has. By the fall of 1990, sales figures for hardcover and paperback titles had climbed to over fifty million, not including *Fudge-a-mania.*

Superfudge, published in 1980, sold over a quarter of a million copies in hardcover within four months, and the paperback edition sold over a million and a half copies in six months. The usual juvenile novel sells only ten to fifteen thousand copies in four or five years.[4]

Blume's first two books, *The One in the Middle Is the Green Kangaroo* (1969) and *Iggie's House* (1970), did not break any sales records. That did not deter Blume, since *Are You There God? It's Me, Margaret.* had already landed on

Dick Jackson's desk. He loved it, as would every fourth, fifth, and sixth grader in the country. Bradbury published *Margaret* in 1970 and quickly followed in 1971 with the book Blume calls its twin, *Then Again, Maybe I Won't.* Both books deal with the age-old problem of growing up. Margaret's major preoccupation is the date of her first menstruation; Tony's (in *Then Again*) is how to camouflage an erection when standing in front of the class. Also in 1971 came *Freckle Juice,* a humorous story for younger children detailing the plight of a boy who has what he considers to be an overdose of freckles and the problems that ensue when he accepts a classmate's advice for getting rid of them.

In 1972 Blume came out with three new titles, two for middle graders and one for young adults. The young adult title, *It's Not the End of the World,* is the story of a young girl's struggle to accept her parents' divorce. *It's Not the End* carried on the momentum that had begun to build with *Margaret* and *Then Again.* But the publication of *Tales of a Fourth Grade Nothing* and *Otherwise Known as Sheila the Great* endowed Blume with permanent hero status among third and fourth graders across the nation. Part of the appeal of Peter (in *Tales*) and Sheila is that they are both characters with whom kids can easily identify. Peter has a little brother, Fudgie, who insists on making Peter's life less than pleasant. Sheila, a minor character in *Tales,* turns out to have her own story to tell: she is afraid of, among other things, dogs, swimming, and strange noises in the family's new (old) house. *Tales* continues to be one of Blume's largest-selling titles. Year after year the struggles between Peter and his terrorizing sibling are retold to yet another generation of youngsters.

In 1974 Blume broke new ground (and old taboos) with the publication of *Deenie,* the story of a young woman who, on the brink of adolescence, develops scoliosis. She continued the upheaval with *Blubber* (1974), a portrayal of the evil that takes place in countless classrooms across the country. Although the kids who had begun reading Blume with

Margaret were ready five years later to read *Forever* (1975), their parents definitely were not. Blume's popularity with readers of all ages had skyrocketed by this time. Fearing repercussions from parents of the younger crowd for the story's sexual explicitness, Bradbury Press labeled the book "adult." This did little to deter the author's millions of fans, who read and reread Katherine's encounters with Ralph, marked the pages, and passed the book on to friends.

By 1977 Blume had eleven titles in print, each one selling better than the one before it. *Starring Sally J. Freedman as Herself* (1977) was a significant book for Blume as it dealt with a time in her life that had been somewhat traumatic for her—namely, the separation from her father. Sally is living in Miami Beach with her brother, mother, and grandmother for the sake of her brother's health while her father, a dentist, remains in New Jersey but visits the family from time to time. The public did not embrace *Sally* the way Blume might have hoped. Still, it was another Judy Blume book, and youngsters devoured it.

Then a terrible thing—at least for Judy Blume's young readers—happened. She left her juvenile audience for another market. *Wifey* (1978) was not merely labeled "adult," it was an actual adult book. Blume says, "I wrote *Wifey* because I felt a great need for change."[5] In the meantime, Blume's younger fans grew impatient. Would there ever be another Blume book for them? The answer came in the form of *Superfudge* (1980), continuing the adventures and misadventures of Peter Hatcher and his younger sibling and adding yet another junior Hatcher, a baby girl, Tootsie. Librarians applauded, children cheered, and booksellers tried in vain to keep their shelves stocked with this new Blume title that was outselling every other Blume title, not to mention every other children's book in stock.

Anything that followed *Superfudge* was bound to be anticlimactic, and it was, but not because of the quality of the writing. *Tiger Eyes* (1981) is one of Blume's finest works, yet it has never achieved the popularity that it deserves. In *Ti-*

ger Eyes, Blume tells the story of Davey, a young woman whose father is shot and killed during a robbery at his convenience store. Davey must work through her own feelings while helping her mother and younger brother traverse their emotional minefields. In 1983, adults got *Smart Women,* a book not only about divorce but about parents falling in love again. Blume sees the book as appealing not only to adults but also to teens who can and should read it to understand divorce from their parents' point of view. On a lighter note, *The Pain and the Great One* appeared in 1984. A story for younger children, it is a fun-loving look at the relationship between an older sister and a youthful sibling.

For the next two years Blume worked on a project that was closer to her heart than almost any other book she has produced. It came out in 1986 as *Letters to Judy: What Your Kids Wish They Could Tell You,* a compilation of letters Blume received from kids during her nearly twenty-year writing career. It is a book, Blume hopes, that youngsters will give to their parents and parents will share with their children.

The year 1987 saw the birth of Blume's first book for older readers since *Tiger Eyes. Just As Long As We're Together* chronicles the ebb and flow of a relationship among three seventh-grade girls. It is a classic tale of the trials of friendship. Norma Jean Sawicki of Orchard Books said that at the 1987 American Booksellers Association some of the booksellers were so happy to see a new Judy Blume book that "they took the galleys back to their hotel rooms and read the book overnight!"[6]

The fall of 1990 was a time of rejoicing for Fudge fans. Ten years after the publication of *Superfudge, Fudge-a-mania* arrived. In this tale, Peter is once again tormented by the antics of his unruly sibling. What's more, his family has decided to share a summer house with Sheila Tubman's family.

Blume's books have won top honors time and time again, most often when the winners were chosen by the children themselves. For example, in 1974 Blume was the first author to receive the Golden Archer Award from the University of Wisconsin–Oshkosh. The recipient of this award is selected through voting by children in grades four to eight. There is no preselected list of nominees as there is with some awards; the children simply vote for their favorite author. It was, not surprisingly, Judy Blume.[7]

In most cases, however, a list of books that children may choose from has been preselected by a committee. *Tales of a Fourth Grade Nothing* and *Superfudge* are safe choices for teachers and librarians, more so than *Deenie* or *Blubber,* so it is not surprising that these books have won the most honors for their author on lists where children are the voters. *Blubber* was chosen, however, for the Young Reader's Choice Award of the Pacific Northwest in 1977. In this contest, children in grades four to eight chose their favorite title from a nominee list of fifteen books that had been "compiled by librarians from suggestions by other librarians and children in the region."[8]

In 1983 Blume received an award that was not based on children's preferences. It was, appropriately, the Garden State Children's Book Award, given by the Children's Services Section of the New Jersey Library Association. The award serves to recognize "books of merit and also popularity with readers in the early and middle grades (2–5)." Awards are selected by a committee of the New Jersey Library Association. The title for which Blume was honored was *Superfudge.*[9]

Another measure of the reading tastes of youngsters is the Children's Choices List, a joint yearly project of the International Reading Association and the Children's Book Council. Approximately 10,000 children from throughout the United States participate in choosing their favorite books published during the previous year. Books are preselected by a committee of educators. *Blubber* was the title chosen in 1974, accompanied by this glowing review: "Here is another favorite from Judy Blume. The book never rests. It talks about childhood cruelty and how it can feel (and how it can backfire). Boys and girls who usually do not read on their own want to read *Blubber*. Children laugh out loud when it's read to them."[10]

In 1982 Barbara Elleman of the American Library Association's *Booklist* magazine conducted a poll of thousands of children across the United States to determine the fifty most popular children's books in the country. The results of the survey were compiled and labeled the "Chosen by Children" list. Four of the top five were Blume titles. *Superfudge* was number one, followed by *Tales of a Fourth Grade Nothing* and *Are You There God? It's Me, Margaret. Charlotte's Web* by E. B. White snuck into the number four spot, and *Blubber* ranked number five. Ten of Blume's books, from *Freckle Juice* to *Forever,* were in the top forty. Some teachers and librarians were distressed by the results of this survey. Others expressed surprise when Blume's books did *not* appear on their students' ballots. Elleman wondered about quality versus popularity as reflected in the polling: "For those who bemoan the lack of quality reading, there are four Newbery winners on the list along with numerous ALA/ALSC Notable Books, two Wilder Award authors, and one Anderson medalist. Popularity does not always, unfortunately, mean high quality—one only needs to check out the *New York Times* best-seller list for a rundown on adult reading patterns. Escape reading—of one's own choice—has a place in children's lives as well as in adults'. The key is to balance it with good literature, sometimes easier to say than do."[11]

There is an unfortunate implication in Elleman's statement that the titles the children chose as their favorites do not conform to the category of good literature. Elleman goes on to say, "In libraries where children's reading interests are promoted and encouraged, authors such as Bellairs, L'Engle, Aiken and Konigsburg got on the ballots, reaffirming the knowledge that children can be led to good literature."[12] The message seems to be that children cannot be trusted to choose good literature on their own. The fact is that children and teens select reading material in a wide range of topics and age levels. Those who are readers gulp down any book they can get their hands on. They may read *Deenie* and *Moby-Dick* at the same sitting. The "Chosen by Children" list is in fact a well-balanced accounting of children's tastes in reading. The tally includes the Little House books, the Lord of the Rings trilogy, several Beverly Cleary titles, the Narnia chronicles, the Nancy Drew and Hardy Boys series, *Charlie and the Chocolate Factory,* and *James and the Giant Peach.*

Dr. Donald Gallo, past president of the Assembly on Literature for Adolescents, emphasizes the need for students to be offered a variety of reading materials and points out once again Blume's popularity in a survey he conducted in 1982. Gallo polled nearly 3,500 students in grades four through twelve in a variety of schools throughout Connecticut and asked them to list up to three of the best books they had read on their own in the previous two years. Students listed Blume more frequently than any other author. "In the fourth grade, sixty percent of the boys and ninety percent of the girls named Blume as their favorite author. . . . More than forty percent of the eighth grade girls and nearly thirty percent of the ninth grade girls listed Blume. In fact, Blume's name topped the list in *every* grade throughout elementary school, through junior high school, and up through grade eleven in our survey."[13] *Are You There God? It's Me, Margaret.* and *Superfudge* topped the list in grades four, five, and six. In grade twelve *Of Mice and Men* by Steinbeck was most often named. In between, the choices included *Where the Red Fern Grows* by Wilson Rawls, V. C. Andrews's *Flowers in the Attic, The Outsiders* by S. E. Hinton, and Harper Lee's *To Kill a Mockingbird.* Gallo points out that students choose a number of different types of books at various points in their reading development and it is to their detriment when we look down our noses at some types of literature as being of inferior quality. In regard to Blume,

Gallo concludes, "There probably hasn't been any other writer in history who has been that popular. We ought to look at why and we ought to learn from it."[14]

One lesson that has been learned over the years is that Blume's words speak not only to the middle-class American child but to children everywhere. "Too American," recalls Claire Smith, Blume's agent. "That's what publishers abroad kept saying. That resistance, however, has broken down over the years as publishers find that her books appeal to almost all youthful readers, no matter what their country of residence."[15] All of Blume's titles have been translated into at least three foreign languages, with *It's Not the End of the World* and *Otherwise Known as Sheila the Great* published in eight different languages.

Blume wonders herself why her books are so well liked. "Why me; why my books?" she asks, genuinely puzzled. Don Gallo attempts to answer the riddle of Blume's popularity. "Judy Blume is not the most popular author alive today just because she looks like a kid. She is popular because *what* she writes about and *how* she writes it make her characters and their actions more real than anything anyone else writes—or perhaps has *ever* written for preteenagers and younger adolescents."[16]

Gallo is not alone in seeking to unravel the mystery of Blume's appeal. Alleen Pace Nilsen and Kenneth L. Donelson, in *Literature for Today's Young Adults,* offers this explanation: "What has made Blume's books so popular is their refreshing candor about worries that young people really do have."[17] Philomena Hauck, in a paper presented to the Canadian Council of Teachers of English, cites another factor that may be even more significant—namely, the books' easy, readable style. Kids who could not begin to complete Dickens or Poe can pick up a Blume title and finish it. According to Hauck's study, "One girl who said she hardly ever read a book through because her brain didn't work when she was reading, enjoyed all of them [Blume's books] because she could follow the story."[18] As Richard Jackson reminds us,

"Judy is very often popular with kids who are not readers, and they are the majority of people on this planet, whether we like it or not." Barbara Gainer Oliver, head children's librarian at the Sante Fe (New Mexico) Public Library sees Blume's ability to "combine humor with realism" as the main factor in her ability to gain and maintain readers. "The children can laugh at themselves through a character, when it would be too painful to laugh at themselves directly."[19]

Barbara Rollock, formerly children's coordinator at the New York Public Library, is struck by Blume's ability to appeal to readers from a variety of ethnic backgrounds and various reading abilities. Rollock feels "her writing cuts across all classes because she talks about the fears and insecurities of childhood." Mary Henry of the South Shore Middle School in Seattle, Washington, agrees and points out that Blume may be using suburban middle-class settings, but her readers are not exclusively suburban middle-class kids. "Special Ed. through gifted, any racial or ethnic background, they all like her. Some of my most alienated, most troubled kids seem to feel that Judy Blume gives them a kind of security."[20]

Richard Jackson reinforces all of these ideas with his own theory about the reason for Blume's success in reaching her readers. "Quite apart from the subject matter, apart from the extraordinary economy of how she gets the stories done, the recognizability of the characters, the real reason for their popularity is that kids are hearing the books, and they're hearing other kids." He goes on to explain that "her books are read by kids who are ostensibly too young for them. But they read them because they're so accessible. I mean, to read them is never a trial, and the reason for that is that the books 'listen' beautifully. I think a kid reading them is actually hearing them."

What kids are hearing is the voice of a (more or less) twelve-year-old. Blume credits a gift of total recall for her ability to transport herself back in time into a youngster's sneakers. But Allen Raymond, editor of *Early Years* magazine, thinks there is more to it than that. He says, "She's gotten inside herself. What is important to her, including her incredibly sensitive feelings, pours out. Children relate to that."[21] Blume offers one possible solution: "I don't understand why I am so successful, except that there must be something I do that makes people see themselves in my stories. I get letters from both kids and adults saying, 'You let me know I am not alone.' "[22]

Blume does get letters, as many as two thousand a month, from her enthusiastic fans. They tell her what they like about her books and what other kinds of books they would like her to write. She tries to reply personally to as many of the letters as possible, especially the ones from young people with problems. The kids themselves can best explain their infatuation with their favorite author. One sixth grader says, "I like Judy Blume because every book she writes about a kid with a problem concerns a little bit of me. . . . It's like she knows me and is writing about me." Another comments simply, "She brings out more me when she writes."[23] Others say, "She writes about people I would like to know," and "She knows what I am like." [24] An eleven-year-old confides that she likes the fact that Blume's books are "about life the way it really is. . . . Some [of her books] just sort of stop and you know things will go on just the way they are."[25]

Blume has gotten inside herself to an honest core. She is honest with her readers, and they identify because they have not yet learned to hide their thoughts and feelings. Blume's honesty is more than merely telling the truth, although that is part of it. Words such as *naïveté* and *candor* come to mind. Blume's characters are sometimes too honest; hearts are worn on sleeves and occasionally broken. Blume's characters also appear to be simple, one-sided, but their simplicity is that of childhood: honest—and complex. Judith Goldberger, in the *Newsletter on Intellectual Freedom,* agrees that honesty is a key factor in Blume's success. However, she concludes, "Her allies . . . would probably agree that it is her honesty which is a large part of what makes her so good to read. But it is also her honesty that makes her opponents so angry with her."[26]

3

"Filth," "Garbage," and "Pornography"

Judy Blume is not only the most popular children's author in the United States, she is also the most censored. According to the liberal group People for the American Way, Blume has topped the list of most banned authors for the last five years, with four of her books among the fourteen most frequently censored titles. The four books to win the honor were, in order, *Deenie, Forever, Blubber,* and *Then Again, Maybe I Won't.*[1]

Dr. Kenneth L. Donelson, professor of English at Arizona State University and co-author of *Literature for Today's Young Adults,* agrees that Blume is the most censored children's author in the United States today. Donelson has followed the rise of censorship in American classrooms for a number of years and in 1985 published an article in *School Library Journal* on book protests in secondary schools from 1972 through 1984. He concluded from his findings that Blume was the second most widely protested author in the country, next to John Steinbeck. The one Blume title that Donelson found to be constantly under attack in junior and senior high schools was *Forever.*

According to Donelson's survey, 1984 was a record year for book protests. His figures show that the number of challenges for *Forever* grew from one in 1980 to twelve in 1984. For *Deenie* the number increased from zero in 1980 to seven in 1984, and for *Then Again* it jumped from one in 1980 to seven in 1984.[2] Overall, says the American Library Association's Office for Intellectual Freedom, the number of reported censorship attempts on all authors rose from three hundred in 1979 to a record one thousand in 1984.[3] Asked if intensified censorship efforts were connected to the political party in power, Maxwell Lillienstein, attorney for the American Booksellers Association, said that "the current administration has given impetus to groups that were dormant."[4] Groups such as the Moral Majority and the Eagle Forum are well known for their censorship efforts, but the 1986 People for the American Way report reveals two new players on the censorship team: the National Association of Christian Educators (NACE) and its activist arm Citizens for Excellence in Education (CEE). The goal of CEE is "to bring public education back under the control of Christians." In 1986–87 the group was involved in twenty-two reported incidents of censorship. They have also been active in running CEE candidates for local school board elections.[5]

Censorship can and does occur in any part of the country, in any school, and in any library. Asked to comment whether there is one area of the country where censorship is more intense than another, Lillienstein said, "It is so pervasive that it would be hard to single out an area."[6] Arthur J. Kropp, PAW executive director, states, "The notion that it's a redneck, rural problem is a myth. Censors in the Midwest, a region considered among the most mature and sophisticated, have the best batting average anywhere."[7] Blume's books have been attacked in Cedar Rapids, Iowa, and Hanover, Pennsylvania; in Montgomery County, Maryland, and Gwinnett County, Georgia; in Del Valle, Texas, and Elk River, Minnesota.

An argument in Blume's *It's Not the End of the World* precipitated the first letters of complaint Richard Jackson received concerning Blume's writing. "The complaints," he says, "centered around language. In one of their fights, the mother calls the father a bastard. I sent out a letter to people who had complained in which I discussed whether a word printed is more terrible than a word heard. It turns out that for many people, it is. If it is in print, it has a kind of validity that the heard word does not." For the author, censorship came earlier and was more devastating. She explains: "When *Margaret* was published, I gave three copies in hardcover to the library at my children's elementary school. They never appeared on the shelf. The male principal wouldn't allow them because the book dealt with menstruation."[8]

Some Blume titles are obvious censor bait: *Deenie, Forever, Then Again, Maybe I Won't.* Occasionally, however, books are placed on a censorship list without any apparent reason. In Casper, Wyoming, in 1985, a group of parents filed a complaint with the school board in which they listed the following Blume titles: *Tiger Eyes, Deenie, Iggie's House, Then Again, Maybe I Won't, Starring Sally J. Freedman as Herself, It's Not the End of the World, Blubber, Superfudge, Otherwise Known as Sheila the Great,* and *The One in the Middle Is the Green Kangaroo.* The complainants said, not surprisingly, that they had not read all the books but had read five or six of them.[9]

Another unique incident in the annals of censorship occurred in Peoria, Illinois, when associate school superintendent Dennis Gainey chose a committee to review three of Blume's books—*Blubber, Deenie,* and *Then Again, Maybe I Won't*—even though no formal complaint had been filed. His comment: "Did we have to do it? No. Do we think it is the prudent thing to do? Yes."[10]

Middle school librarian Elyse Clark would not agree. Clark filed a grievance with the Pennsylvania State Education Association when five Blume titles and Norma Klein's *Honey of a Chimp* were removed from the Hanover Public School District's elementary and middle school libraries and placed on a "restricted shelf." When parent Jeffrey Hoffheins originally complained about the Klein book, he wrote at the bottom of the form, "Recommend reviewing all Judy Blume books for similar content."[11] Clark maintained that since no formal complaint of the Blume titles had been received, there was no justification for removing them.

Like Hoffheins, Joan and Peter Podchernikoff of the Cotati-Rohnert Park, California, school district, believed that they should be able to control not only their own child's reading habits, but those of every child in the district. In August of 1982 they requested that the school board remove *Deenie* from all district schools. The board appointed a committee to review the book. That was not unusual. What was unusual, however, in this case was that before the committee's report was submitted, board member Andy Camozzi proposed a general ban on all Blume titles until each could be reviewed by the board itself. "Some of these books are pornography," Camozzi said. "We might as well put *Playgirl* and *Playboy* magazines in the library."[12]

Parents and school officials are not the only ones to involve themselves in the censorship fray. Frequently ministers or other religious leaders will initiate a complaint on behalf of a group. In 1985 in Cedar Rapids, Iowa, Timothy Stafford, administrator of the Cedar Rapids Christian School, asked the public library's board of trustees to remove copies of *Forever* from its shelves. The book was shelved in the adult section of the library and had been found in the school's locker room by a staff member.[13]

Finally, in what is probably the longest-running censorship debate in history, a member of the Gwinnett County, Georgia, chapter of Citizens for Excellence in Education asked in 1985 to have copies of *Deenie* removed from elementary school libraries. Words flew in seemingly endless debate, the ACLU was brought in, and eventually the book was removed from the elementary schools but retained in the middle and high schools. At last word, the controversy was not over yet.[14]

Parents, religious leaders, even teachers, school board members, and administrators complain. In the case of the Blume books, the objections generally focus on three areas: sex, which in the mind of the censor includes masturbation, menstruation, sex education, and actual sex; "strong language," which again can cover a multitude of alleged sins; and "lack of moral tone."

The latter, lack of moral tone, has come to be a catch phrase among right-wing religious groups denoting any work to which they object. The group Pro-Family Forum, in a pamphlet entitled "X-Rated Children's Books," attacks *Blubber* for its alleged lack of moral guidance, citing passages detailing "How to Have Fun with Blubber." The group concludes that since the author does not state plainly that this behavior on the part of the children is malicious, she is therefore endorsing their activity as right and proper.[15] Quite the opposite is, in fact, true.

Blume hopes that when children read her books they think about the actions of the characters. She does not give them the answers to their moral questions but expects them to exercise their own thought processes. Pro-Family Forum finds considerable fault with that approach. Allowing children to think for themselves is what they term the "new morality" and "values clarification." "This concept," they argue, "leaves young people in a fluid state, with no moral or spiritual guidelines, and unusually sensitive to, and molded by, all surrounding influences."[16] The Pro-Family Forum mentality does not respect the child's ability to reason and arrive at correct answers without heavy-handed adult supervision and control.

Dorothy Broderick, editor of *Voice of Youth Advocates,* provides a possible answer to *why* some individuals are threatened by a lack of rigid moral guidelines. She says, "Human beings *need* to feel in control, and, since we live in a world where the large issues are beyond our control, we search for ways to prove to ourselves that we have some measure of control over our existence. . . . We cannot protect our youth from the great threats of society, so we turn to protecting them in the only areas in which we have any sense of control at all—we direct our energies at censoring what young people will be allowed to read, hear, and view."[17]

Blume comments, "They [censors] think that by burying the issue they can control their child's thought. If I don't expose my child to this, they think, then my child is not going to think about this. That is not the way it works."[18]

Norma Klein, well-known and often-censored author of books for children and young adults, said, "One of the fears is that children will do what they read about in books. This fear is based on the false belief that children would never have had the thought without the book. They would never have thought about masturbating, say, but the second they read about it, that's all they'll do. Maybe they'll never practice the piano again!"[19]

The effect of the censor is being felt in schools throughout the United States. Textbooks, particularly reading texts, that were on their way to becoming interesting for children, have had to be "dumbed down" because certain ideas are offensive to some people. But every idea is insulting to someone. Blume has said, "There are certain books around that make me cringe, too—I hate the written-to-order romances—but I would never forbid my child or anyone else's to read them. I would just make them aware of what else is available."[20] "Children are their own best censors," according to Blume. "What matters is that they continue to have a choice. It is up to us to provide them with a balanced diet. But if reality is removed from their diet, if they are not encouraged to face it as children, how can we expect them to cope as adults?"[21]

Blume "insists she purposely takes *no* moral stand, that the danger of moralizing in a realistic story is that there usually are no purely 'right' answers. To claim that there are is to set guidelines that may not stand up to the test of reality."[22] Another popular author of realistic fiction for young people, Robert Cormier, in answering criticism of his book *The Chocolate War,* says, "I was trying to write realistically even though I knew it would upset some young people. The fact is that the good guys don't always win in real life and I wanted to show that."[23]

Richard Jackson finds it ludicrous that anyone would find

Blume's books "lacking in moral tone." He says, "I think there is a morality that runs through all the books. I think all her books imply something about kindliness . . . in a variety of ways." Judith Krug, director of the Office for Intellectual Freedom of the American Library Association, agrees. "When I hear people say Judy Blume is immoral . . . it really bothers me. She's probably one of the most moral writers for children and young people, which is exactly why she's so popular. She's writing for them in their language, dealing with their problems in a totally noncondescending way. She's saying you're human, you have problems and your problems are going to change as you get older. But that's not going to make your current problems less painful."[24] Blume displays a morality in her writing in other ways, too, as librarian Barbara Ann Porte points out. "Perhaps surprisingly to some adults, in view of some of the issues Blume raises in her work, the books remain strongly supportive of most traditional values. Her main characters don't smoke, drink, or take drugs. Honesty, especially in relationship to one's parents, is strongly encouraged. Her characters generally seem to want to do what's right, and, like most of us, hope that doing so won't turn out to be too inconvenient."[25]

Let us not be lulled into thinking that it is only the conservatives who have led the attack against Blume's writing. Liberals have also gotten into the act. Certain members of the women's movement have attacked Blume's writing on the grounds that it lacks a "feminist perspective." The anonymous author of an article in *Interracial Books for Children Bulletin* writes: "With the exception of *Deenie,* her perspective seems to be virtually untouched by the women's movement. . . . Although six of Blume's eight main characters are girls, not one fights the feminist fight—that is, struggles consciously to change the second-class status of her girlhood."[26] Blume answers that charge in an interview with Audrey Eaglen in *Top of the News.* She says, "I'm a story teller. . . . I won't always paint characters who are waving the flag, unless that's part of the story I'm telling."[27]

Blume does allow that, were she writing *Are You There God?* today, the mother would probably be working. Although Blume herself did not leave the house for a job, she was definitely a working mother. She does not talk much about her politics, but on women's issues she says, "I am a feminist. . . . My own struggle, my own need for meaningful work outside the family, before I ever heard of the women's movement, was a real problem. . . . I saw my first marriage go under and I know my first husband blames it on my work. . . . For my daughter, I know what I want, but she has to make her own choices, and I want those choices to be available to her."[28]

In the same *Interracial Books for Children* article, Blume is labeled a racist. The author points out that the Miglione family of *Then Again, Maybe I Won't* is Italian and the Garbers in *Iggie's House* are black, but "the only other ethnic representations are half-Jewish Margaret, Deenie's Jewish girl friend and the Chinese-American girl friend in *Blubber.*"[29] Blume says that Dorothy Broderick is reported to have defended the author at an American Library Association meeting with a statement to the effect that she writes what she knows. She grew up in suburban New Jersey, argued Broderick, therefore it is logical that she writes about suburban New Jersey. Richard Jackson presents a similar argument when he says, "Judy doesn't know anything about a traveling circus—unless she's hiding something from me—and I wouldn't expect her to set any of her books in a traveling circus." As Judith M. Goldberger writes in the *Newsletter on Intellectual Freedom,* "The issue, according to Blume, is control. If critics would have her change the content of her books, adding moral judgments, or even altering racial, sexual, or economic class backdrops, they would deny the writer's right to speak personally, and hence, from the heart."[30]

The four Blume titles that censors continue to focus on

are *Blubber, Deenie, Forever,* and *Then Again, Maybe I Won't.* In 1987 a parent in Muskego, Wisconsin, filed a complaint with the library board regarding *Blubber.* The parent objected to the story "because the characters curse and the leader of the taunting is never punished for her cruelty." [31] (Jill's mother does say "damn" when she gets a run in her pantyhose as she is rushing to get dressed, Jill's father says "damn it" when he is angry, and Jill *thinks* "Damn that Blubber! . . . It's all her fault," when Miss Rothbelle reprimands her.) Again, the "lack of moral tone" was alluded to by a parent in Montgomery County, Maryland, in 1980. Bonnie Fogel filed a complaint with the school district in regard to *Blubber,* stating, "There's no adult or another child at the end who says, 'This is wrong. This cruelty to others shouldn't be.' " [32] In Del Valle, Texas, in 1983 a teacher requested the removal of *Blubber* from the elementary school library shelves because of "inappropriate language." She claimed that the book had a disruptive effect on her fourth-grade class. "It was passed around and the words were underlined. It was for shock effect." [33] Both *It's Not the End of the World* and *Blubber* came under fire from the Lindenwold, New Jersey, Board of Education because of "a problem with language." Said Superintendent of Schools Edward Zinpol, "We thought the books had a moral message. They did have integrity. But there was a problem with the language. We're not a public library." *Blubber* was removed from the shelves of the Lindenwold elementary school libraries and is available to the sixth-graders by request. *It's Not the End of the World* is available only to students in grades four through six. [34]

When in 1985 Timothy Stafford asked the Cedar Rapids, Iowa, public library board to remove *Forever* from the shelves, he called the book "pornography" with "no literary value" and charged that it "explores areas God didn't intend to explore outside of marriage." [35] In the 1983 Cotati-Rohnert Park School District case, Joan and Peter Podchernikoff asked the school board to remove *Deenie* from school libraries. According to Joan Podchernikoff, Blume's writing "titillates" and "stimulates" children "to the point they could be prematurely awakened sexually." The Podchernikoffs objected specifically to the passage in *Deenie* describing masturbation.[36] (Deenie's words: "As soon as I got into bed I started touching myself. I have this special place and when I rub it I get a very nice feeling. I don't know what it's called or if anyone else has it but when I have trouble falling asleep, touching my special place helps a lot.") Joan Podchernikoff said, "These are things she [her daughter] really doesn't understand. These are things we want to tell her, not Judy Blume." The couple concluded, "You have to draw the line somewhere. If you don't legislate morality, you are legislating immorality."[37] In 1982 three angry parents in Scranton, Pennsylvania, demanded that *Forever* be banned from the Midvalley Junior–Senior High School library. The parents spoke up at a school board meeting, calling the book "filth," "garbage," and "pornography" and said it contained "four-letter words and talked about masturbation, birth control, and disobedience to parents."[38] (The four-letter words occur when Katherine's younger sister asks her what she and Michael were doing in the bedroom. "Were you fucking?" . . . "That's not a bad word . . . hate and war are bad words but fuck isn't.")

The 1985 Peoria, Illinois, case attacked three of Blume's most popular titles, *Blubber, Deenie,* and *Then Again, Maybe I Won't,* because of their "sexual content, strong language, and alleged lack of social or literary value." Sherry Mermis, a parent who had complained when the books were removed from school shelves, said, "The story content of those books has a lot to say to children."[39] The Peoria incident also garnered anticensorship support from well-known children's authors Natalie Babbitt, Virginia Hamilton, Madeleine L'Engle, Milton Meltzer, Katherine Paterson, Uri Schulevitz, Elizabeth George Speare, and William Steig.[40] The Gwinnett County, Georgia, case involving *Deenie* began in 1985 with a complaint from Theresa Wilson, the mother of a nine-year-old girl. Wilson protested that the book was "pornography," saying, "You don't have to read the whole book. Trash is trash, doesn't matter what else is in the book."[41] She went on to charge that *Deenie* contained "frank discussions of masturbation, menstruation, and sexual intercourse."[42] It could be argued that *Deenie* contains "frank discussions of masturbation," but menstruation and sexual intercourse are mentioned only in passing.

Those who speak in favor of removing books from public and school libraries often speak the loudest. Yet there have been occasions where parents have risen in support of the allegedly offensive material. In Gwinnett County, Christine Winokur, a member of the anticensorship group, told the press, "I became outraged that some people would tell the community they were more moral and that their idea of morality would prevail. They want to take control of public education and turn it into private education."[43] With threats of removing *Are You There God?* and *Blubber* ringing in her ears, Xenia, Ohio, resident Marilyn McKeown told fellow parents: "Students should be taught how to read and write and reason, not what to read or write or think."[44] In Elk River, Minnesota, the mother of a fourth-grade student threatened to sue school officials over restrictions placed on books in school libraries. The restricted titles included *Are You There God?*, *Deenie,* and *Then Again, Maybe I Won't.*[45]

Parents who raise the issue of removing books from school or public libraries are, given the benefit of the doubt, concerned, caring parents. However, what many of them do not seem to understand is that because the book is there, it does not have to be read. They can control their child's reading like they control the "off" button on the television set. But, they will argue, what if my child reads the book, and I am not aware of it. What will happen to the child?

There are those who feel we must "save the children." What, indeed, are we saving them from? The four-letter words? They have heard them all. The fact that there is evil in the world that sometimes goes unpunished? If they have an older brother or sister, they know that too. Sex? It is a difficult secret to keep. Why do the censors go after the "bad words?" Because it is easy. The words are obvious to pick out, and it is then comfortable to feel like a good parent, a parent who is concerned about one's children. The fact is, it is not that simple to be a parent, let alone a good one, but the answer lies not in censoring every word the child reads but in listening to what the child has to say. Librarians and media specialists, too, could benefit from a short course on listening to youngsters and understanding their needs.

In an interpretation of the Library Bill of Rights aimed at defining free access to libraries for minors, the American Library Association wrote in April 1984 regarding material selection decisions that "restrictions are often initiated under the assumption that certain materials may be 'harmful' to minors, or in an effort to avoid controversy with parents. Libraries or library boards who would restrict the access of minors to materials and services because of actual or suspected parental objections should bear in mind that they do not serve *in loco parentis.*" [46]

Another statement by the American Library Association elaborates on the theme of *in loco parentis:*

> In our society, the primary responsibilities involved in rearing children rest with parents. The Supreme Court has asserted that governmental agencies neither can nor should attempt to fulfill certain parental obligations to the child. Various public institutions, including schools, foster the well-being of children and thereby serve the public good. But the activities of such institutions must be consistent with the fulfillment of parental duties. If there are certain ideas, certain works, that a parent wishes to keep from his child, he should assume the task of shielding his child. Any sweeping ban on ideas or works which he deems harmful to his child would clearly infringe on the rights of other parents to introduce their children to precisely those ideas and works. [47]

A separate statement entitled "Free Access to Information for Young Adults," prepared by the board of directors of the Intellectual Freedom Committee of the Young Adult Services Division, defines further the rights of teens in regard to libraries. "Young adults have the right to free access to all information in all formats. Librarians have the responsibility to insure this access."[48]

Gwinnett County school board member Bob Wood was not thinking of the rights of young people when he said, "This is not a book-banning issue, this is a parents' control issue. We have to do what parents want."[49] It is easy to buckle under pressure when several angry voices are aimed at one's head. *Deenie* was ultimately removed from the district's elementary school libraries; however, the school board rejected a proposal by parent Theresa Wilson to establish restricted shelves in all district libraries.[50] In Peoria, Illinois, the school trustees voted to lift the ban on *Then Again, Deenie,* and *Blubber.* However, their decision mandates that in Peoria the three Blume titles may not be read by students below the seventh grade.[51] In Elk River, Minnesota, the school board returned the three Blume titles to the school library's shelves when it found that it had not followed the guidelines for removing books set forth by the court in the 1982 Island Trees case.[52] The Loveland, Colorado, board of education cast a unanimous vote to allow unrestricted access to the nine Blume titles in its school libraries. According to a report, "The Board's new policy on the Blume books allows parents who object to a given title to restrict their child's access with a written note." Dave Leech, director of elementary education for the district, said, "They [school board members] felt the burden should be put on the shoulders of the parents who don't want their children reading the books rather than on the majority of parents."[53] In Cotati, California, *Deenie* was retained in the junior and senior high schools and is available to elementary school pupils with parental permission. "In an effort to avoid future controversy," the trustees adopted a new review policy allowing parents to examine all new books purchased at the elementary school level the first two weeks of each month. Parents who object to a title can ask a special committee to review the book, but the principal will make the final decision. However, if a parent is not pleased with the principal's decision, he or she can appeal to the board of trustees.[54] The Muskego, Wisconsin, school board voted six to one to uphold a library committee's recommendation to retain *Blubber* on the shelves.[55] Finally, in Cedar Rapids, Iowa, twenty people on the reconsideration committee and the library board read the entire book *Forever* and all asked that it be retained. The board voted unanimously to keep the book in the library's young adult section. Said board president, Jerry Elsea, "It's something that should be in our collection."[56]

Blume is one of the most popular writers for kids today, and she is—perhaps consequently—one of the most censored. Richard Jackson believes that Blume is prey to criticism that other writers slip past. Why? "Because she's popular," he declares simply. "She's visible, and she's proven her lack of trustworthiness by being so loved by kids." Placing tongue in cheek, he continues, "We all know that kids are terrific, but they have no judgment. Right? Of course that's wrong, but it is one of the assumptions: that if a child really likes a book, it can't be good with a capital G."

"What critics think about Judy and what kids think about her," says Richard Jackson, "is a dichotomy we have lived with for a long time."[57] Youngsters in some cases have stood up to authorities in defense of their beloved author. Blume's favorite example is the case in Loveland, Colorado, of a sixth-grade girl who circulated a petition and collected ninety-five signatures from her classmates in order to keep Blume titles on her school library's shelves. She then went before the school board and made an impassioned plea on behalf of the books. The board was impressed and voted unanimously to allow unrestricted access to the nine Judy

Blume titles in its school libraries.[58] When Blume books were removed from elementary school shelves in Hanover, Pennsylvania, students circulated the following petition: "We understand there has been some book banning in the Hanover Public School District and we would like to protest this action. Most of the Judy Blume books have been taken out of the library and we feel people should be able to read her books or those of any other author. We would like to have these books put back. Book banning seems to be the opposite of the purpose of education."[59] An eleven-year-old girl wrote Blume saying, "Kids are not dumb. We know what is right and wrong. If you want to encourage kids to read, don't take the books we love off the shelves. No book has ever made me do something that I didn't want to do." A twelve-year-old boy asks, "How can they expect us kids to learn anything if they don't let us read stories that tell about life the way it really is?"[60]

Blume says that she deals with the criticism of her books by "not internalizing it. I pretend they're talking about someone else." Her son Larry says, "It bothers her that the extremist groups exist. Their criticisms don't particularly bother her." Blume says that she will never stop fighting censorship, not only of her own books but of any book. "What encourages me," she says, "is the resistance to censorship. . . . It's wonderful to see how local people who love to read will stand up and fight the censors."[61] Blume has appeared on numerous talk shows to discuss the issue of censorship. When she participated in a panel discussion on the Phil Donahue show, she asked, "Who is on the kids' side? Where are the kids and why are they not sitting here with us today? Because it's their rights we're talking about, and their lives and their education, and their reality."[62]

Blume has done more than mouth slogans. She has put money where her convictions are. In 1981 she established the KIDS Fund for the purpose of assisting nonprofit organizations to develop programs that encourage communication between parents and teens and foster parent–child discussion through books. Thus far money has been awarded to projects dealing with sexuality education, teenage pregnancy prevention, child abuse, and problems relating to families under stress. Recently, however, as proof of her faith in young people, she awarded a KIDS Fund grant to a teenager who operates a hotline for youngsters who are home alone after school. Blume has said, "My basic way of dealing with censorship was by starting the KIDS Fund. . . . I believe that censorship grows out of fear, and fear comes from the adult who is insecure about talking about certain issues with the child and so finds it easier to say *no* than to let it come out in the open."[63]

Blume has stated repeatedly that kids will censor their own reading and points to letters from kids who say, "I started to read *Wifey,* but I don't think I'm ready for it." "It is this faith in her readers," one critic has pointed out, "that enables Blume to establish the kind of trust she and her fans have for each other."[64] In a panel discussion with school board members and educators from across the country, Blume remarked, "More and more I'm counting on my readers to come to the defense of my books."[65]

4

Truth and Consequences

"Sybil Davison has a genius I.Q. and has been laid by at least six different guys." This opening line from *Forever* is one of the most talked about, most disputed, most controversial sentences in all young adult literature, and it adds fuel to the controversy about the rest of the book, since many adults are not able to get past the word *laid*. It is a grabber of a sentence, but does it, as one critic has claimed, set the tone for the entire book?[1] Blume explains, "What I was trying to say in *Forever* was that a girl like Sybil might have a genius IQ but she has no common sense."

Katherine, the main character, is, in comparison with Sybil, much more thoughtful in her actions. She does not merely want to "get laid." In fact, we know quite early in the story that she stopped seeing Tommy Aronson when she realized that "sex was all he was ever interested in, which is why we broke up—because he threatened that if I wouldn't sleep with him he'd find somebody who would."

Blume explains how *Forever* came to be written. "Randy was fourteen and reading all the 'pregnant' books—*Mr. & Mrs. Bo Jo Jones,* and others. In these books, the boys had absolutely no feelings, and the girl 'did it' not because she was excited sexually, but because she was mad at her parents. And she was always punished for it." As authors Myra and David Sadker point out in comparing *Forever* to other books about teenage sex, "In *Mr. & Mrs. Bo Jo Jones* and *Too Bad About the Haines Girl* the culprit was liquor. . . . Anger and spite toward a third party are offered as the cause in *My Darling, My Hamburger* and *Bonnie Jo, Go Home.*"[2] Blume's intent was to write a story about a girl of average intelligence who makes a rational decision to have sex with her boyfriend and who does not have to suffer dire consequences or punishment. As is true of many of her other books, Blume also wrote *Forever* to satisfy a need for a book she wished she had had as a young woman growing up. She says, "I wish someone had told me, 'This is what sex might be like.' "[3]

Forever is Katherine's story. Michael, of course, is a main character, as is a part of Michael's body, which he introduces to her as Ralph. Katherine's friend Erica and Michael's friend Artie are secondary characters, as is Sybil, at whose house Katherine and Michael meet. Michael's sister Sharon and her husband, Ike, are also minor characters; the couple's ski cabin and their apartment are the sites of most of Michael and Katherine's sexual encounters. Katherine's relationship with her parents is significant as is her relationship with her younger sister, Jamie. Katherine's grandmother also plays a vital role in the story.

Katherine Danziger is seventeen and a senior in high school. At a New Year's Eve party, Katherine meets Michael Wagner. They are attracted to each other. They ski together, they wash dishes together, and soon they are in bed together. Kath asks Michael to wait, and he does. She wants to be "mentally ready" as well as physically ready. After several weeks of deliberation, Katherine gives up her virginity, willingly and with love. But nothing is forever, and when Katherine meets and likes a young man at summer camp, she ends her relationship with Michael.

Michael is a sensitive young man who is deeply hurt when the relationship dissolves. "He went into the bathroom, slammed the door and flushed the toilet so I couldn't hear anything." Presumably Michael is crying. Blume says, "I set out to teach very few things in my books, but I did set out in *Forever* to show that boys can love just as hard, feel just as much pain."[4] Michael seems to need Katherine's love more than she needs his. He is the one who suggests that their love will last forever. Katherine is part of an extremely loving family and thus is fairly secure about herself. We know little about Michael's parents, other than that they are "a little stuffier" than Katherine's. Michael, however, is more emotionally insecure than Katherine and, in general, more immature—witness the way he drives off spinning his tires following the breakup. As critic John Gough suggests, "Neither Kath nor Michael are yet mature enough to continue with friendship once they stop loving."[5]

Katherine suffers too as she sees her relationship with Michael dissolving and her relationship with her new friend Theo growing. In a letter she writes to Michael, trying to explain that her feelings have changed, she says, "You must be thinking what a rotten person I am. Well, believe me, I'm thinking the same thing. . . . I don't want to hurt you . . . not ever. . . ." She is crying as she writes the letter, and she blames herself, wondering, "Maybe there's something wrong with me." Katherine is not insensitive to Michael's feelings. Yet she realizes that she is not ready for forever, and there is a feeling that she may not agree to forever as easily the next time. Katherine has grown from her experience with Michael and not merely sexually. Michael may or may not have learned anything.

Katherine has a good support system (and excellent role models) in her family. She says of her parents, "My mother and father are certainly the happiest married couple I know." The Danzigers are a close-knit family. They do things together such as rug-hooking, and when Katherine is sick with the flu her parents take turns staying home with her, even though she is quite old enough to stay by herself. Katherine, in turn, is caring and considerate of her younger sister. She feels especially protective when her relationship with Michael intensifies, and she realizes that Jamie is looking to her as a role model.

In *Forever* it is Katherine's grandmother who sends her information about Planned Parenthood. Grandparents, especially grandmothers, figure prominently in several of Blume's novels. In *Fudge-a-mania*, Grandma Muriel is a retired gymnast, but she can still turn a mean cartwheel. She also senses how Peter is feeling when she asks, "It's not easy being the firstborn, is it?" Margaret's grandmother in *Are You There God? It's Me, Margaret.* brings her deli food and takes her on outings to Lincoln Center. Both Tony's grandmother in *Then Again* and Sally's grandmother in *Starring Sally J. Freedman* are from the old world. Both grandmothers are warm and loving, and both Tony and Sally share feelings with their grandmothers that they cannot share with their mothers. Blume says, "Grandmothers can often offer insights because they are in a way removed from the immediate problem." She says that she writes about grandmothers because she hopes one day to be the kind of active grandmother portrayed in her books.

Blume also says that she identifies strongly with Katherine's mother. "Not that I don't identify with Katherine, but I could see myself as Katherine's mother, and I like her." Mrs. Danziger perhaps is the children's librarian that Blume secretly longed to be.

The Danzigers love their daughters: they respect them and trust their judgment. In a frank discussion about sex, Mrs. Danziger tells Katherine, "I'm not going to tell you to go ahead, but I'm not going to forbid it either. . . . I expect you to handle it with a sense of responsibility, though . . . either way."

Katherine does take responsibility for her body. After her grandmother sends her birth control information, she makes an appointment at the Planned Parenthood Clinic. She is given a pelvic exam and a prescription for birth control pills. It is all very matter-of-fact. Even before she goes to the clinic, Katherine insists that Michael use a condom during their lovemaking. As Patty Campbell points out, "The incident is a strong example for girls who might otherwise choose the risk of pregnancy over the risk of social embarrassment."[6]

The descriptions of birth control methods and of Katherine and Michael's lovemaking have caused the book to be both decried and praised as a sex education guide. One critic described it as "a manufactured sex manual thinly disguised as a novel."[7] Lou Willett Stanek called it "a problem novel . . . that is as explicit as a sex manual."[8]

Although Blume did not write the book as a sex education treatise, she did write it to provide information, as she does in all her writing. Pamela Pollock, in *Siecus Report,* commends this approach: "Potentially, children's fiction dealing with sexual themes can answer the same questions as nonfiction on the topic, and do so in a more immediate and involving way. Thus it presents a great opportunity not only to provide young people with scientific facts about sex, but also to deal with the emotional and attitudinal concerns that young people have about their own sexuality."[9]

As Faith McNulty explains, "Blume's description of what Katherine and Michael do in bed, and what Katherine feels, is a carefully worded answer to questions hygiene manuals fail to address."[10] In fact, a teacher in a California school used the book to impart the "feelings aspect" in a sex education class. She said, "By using a novel such as *Forever* you can tie in all the anatomy and physiology that you teach in the course with the sexual decision-making that kids must experience." She goes on: "Kids are told, be careful, you'll get V.D., but nobody ever says, be careful, you'll get your feelings hurt."[11]

Those who oppose sex education in the first place oppose it even more in a fictional format. Basically, they argue that if kids read about it, they are going to do it. As one concerned parent argues, "Maybe I'm out of it, but doggone it, this is how I feel. The Scriptures say premarital sex is wrong. Then Judy Blume comes along and writes about it and it starts seeming like the norm."[12]

Blume contends that *Forever* is a good tool to use in discussing sexuality with young people. She says, "I also get letters from parents. Many times they thank me for writing books that introduce sexuality topics, saying that my books have helped them initiate discussions with their own children."[13] Jean Fredricks, mother of four and former high school sex education instructor, talked of her experience with *Forever*. "My twelve-year-old daughter brought the book home and said, 'Mom, I think this is written by a different Judy Blume. I don't think you should read it.'" Did she read it? "Of course I read it," she said, "and my daughter and I discussed it. I thought it was good because she talks about sex in a very realistic way. It's not all peaches and cream, and yet she's not advocating that every teenager go out and have sex."[14] Dr. Mary Calderone's review of *Forever* in *Siecus* reinforces this point: "Discussing life as it is, in thoughtful, nonargumentative, and mutually respectful fashion, is the best thing parents and children can do today, and a starter would be for all concerned to read this book."[15]

The case has also been made that the young people in the book do give some thought to their actions. Certainly Katherine does not leap into bed with Michael the first time the thought of sleeping with him enters her head. She waits until she feels she is ready. Blume said she could have just as easily written a book in which the girl said no. Her point is that no matter which decision is made, it must be thought out and it must feel right. One teenager says, "The book *Forever* shows a girl making a hard decision. Every girl has to make that decision at one time or another and so Kathy is like a lot of girls I know. My friends don't talk about it though, so it's good to read about someone else's decision. I think it helps."[16]

Blume admits that she has become more conservative over the years regarding kids and sex. "Kids say to me, how old should I be to have intercourse. I tell them to wait until they are out of high school. You can't say what's right for everyone."

With her own children, Blume practiced what she preached and gave them books on sex. Larry Blume recalls, "I remember the first book we had about sex. I must have been seven or eight. It had cutout pictures. We shared it with all the kids in the neighborhood." He goes on, "By fourth grade I was quite the expert on how babies are made. At lunch one day a boy said that babies were made by God sprinkling dust on the mother's tummy. I argued with him, and he started crying. His parents became upset and called the school. The school called my mother and said, 'Cool it.'" Larry says he always felt he could talk to his mother about sex. Judy's daughter Randy concurs that "the Blume children always had books." "We told all our friends the facts," she says, "and we had the books to prove them."

Blume obviously dealt honestly with her own children regarding the facts of life. She not only touts honesty, she lives it. She says, "The more open, the more honest we are with our kids, the better they're going to be able to cope with life."[17] Michael and Katherine talk about being honest with each other. Rather, he talks about it, and she agrees. One evening, following a minor squabble, he says, "From now on we're honest with each other. If something's bothering you, say it, and I'll do the same . . . agreed?"

Katherine and Michael's friends Erica and Artie spend a lot of time playing board games and talking. Artie admits to Erica that he is afraid of having sex with her and that he also fears that he might be homosexual. Erica tells Katherine, "At least we're getting honest with each other . . . and you can't have a decent relationship without honesty."

Erica might also have said that a good relationship requires laughter and playfulness. Katherine and Michael are frolicsome in the beginning stages of their relationship. In an early chapter, they wash dishes together and end up hurling soap suds at each other. Later, when they go on their ski weekend, Katherine gets out of the car and Michael pelts her with snowballs. It is this kind of fun-loving give and take that makes any relationship intriguing. Erica does say, during one of her and Katherine's discussions about sex, that it is important to be friends as well as lovers because "you can't just have sex all day long."

Katherine and Michael do become friends. She speaks of

him as her very best friend. "Besides everything else he is really my best friend now. It's a different kind of friendship from the one I have with Erica. It makes me wish I could share everyday with him—forever."

Yet it seems, as the story progresses, that the more time Katherine and Michael spend in bed together, the less time they spend talking to each other. Near the end of the story, their relationship is almost totally sexual. They skip school to spend the day in bed together. Before they both leave for their summer jobs, they spend the night on the beach together and watch the sun come up, but there is little indication that any fun is involved in the experience. This is the beginning of the end of the relationship.

Early in the story, before the relationship becomes sexual, Katherine tells Michael about her feelings regarding her paternal grandmother and old people in general. Here she shares with Michael something extremely personal about herself. She says, "I never really knew my grandmother . . . as a person, that is, . . . she was just some old lady with crooked fingers and wrinkled skin and I was kind of afraid of her . . . and of other old people, too. . . ." Katherine tells Michael that this is why she volunteers in the geriatric section of the hospital.

In a later book, *Tiger Eyes,* Davey volunteers in a hospital to help herself overcome her fears regarding the elderly. Blume is telling us something about both characters. Katherine in *Forever* and Davey in *Tiger Eyes* are aware of some of their own weaknesses and they make an attempt to correct them. Throughout the book Katherine is in charge of her life—to the extent an eighteen-year-old person can be in charge. When she tells Michael's uncle that her goal in life is to be happy and "make other people happy, too," she is not being frivolous. She knows herself well enough to know that this is what she wants. *Forever* has been called a modern version of Maureen Daly's *Seventeenth Summer.* Blume takes the love story beyond romance to "what really happened." Katherine is not swept off her feet, despite the fact that she does care about Michael intensely. In comparing *Forever* to today's teen romances, Patty Campbell notes, "Instead of promoting the preservation of virginity, the teen romances probably contribute more to its loss than realistic novels like *Forever,* in which girls are shown to be in charge of their own sexuality."[18] Critic John Gough aptly identifies the theme of *Forever* as "directing one's life and accepting the consequences."[19]

There are, of course, librarians, teachers, and reviewers who cannot see beyond Katherine and Michael in bed or beyond Sybil getting laid. Blume feels that too much has been made of the sexuality in the book. "I don't think the sexuality is as important as adults try to make it," she says. Though she would not deny, of course, that the book deals with sexuality, she says that what it is about is making thoughtful choices regarding your life and taking responsibility for those choices.

Forever is not a book that elicits ambivalent feelings. Dorothy Nimmo in the *School Librarian* called it pornographic. "All the right messages are put over, about responsibility and birth-control and not having abortions and illegitimate babies, but all the same I think it is pornography."[20] Audrey Eaglen tells of a branch librarian who "refuses to purchase copies of . . . *Forever* because, . . . he 'will not have such filth in my library.' "[21] He is not alone. British critic David Rees claims that Blume is not in touch with teenagers' feelings. "She has little idea, it seems, of what really occurs, emotionally, in adolescent sexual relationships, either in real life or in the teenage novel."[22]

Nicholas Tucker, agreeing with his countryman Rees's assessment of the book wrote, "The characters are so flat one might almost be in a sexed-up Enid Blyton plot—*Five Go on an Orgy,* perhaps. But at least Enid Blyton sometimes dealt with feelings."[23] Chris Kloet, on the other hand, a British young people's librarian, called the book "a refreshingly honest, humorous guide for survival"[24] and "a straightforward love story which is particularly good for the frank, unsentimental way in which it deals with sex."[25]

Like many of Blume's other works, *Forever* has been faulted for its middle-class setting. Frank Bataglia, a college professor who used the book in a freshman composition class says, "My main problem with the book concerns the narrowness of its class perspective. Almost everyone seems obliviously affluent, with neither money worries nor ambitions." He goes on, "Not every woman who might give up a baby for adoption, like Sybil, can start a new life by going off to college."[26] This is true. However, as Dr. Mary Calderone points out, "Here is how the counselors, clergymen, and physicians who ultimately meet these sexually active and often pregnant teenage girls know it is, in very well-written and graphic form, but in good taste, for after all, it is about nice children from nice families—like yours and mine!"[27] Barbara Rollock, of the New York Public Library, says that Blume's writing cuts across class lines and that her books are read by young people of all ethnic backgrounds and every economic level.

The big question regarding *Forever*, though, is, for what age group was it written? The book jacket reads, "Judy Blume's first novel for adults." But Blume says, *"Forever* is a book I wrote with readers in mind . . . that were 13 and 14, to read before they were actually of the age when they might be acting it out."[28] The answer, most likely, is that the publisher was playing it safe. As Alleen Pace Nilsen notes in the second edition of *Literature for Today's Young Adults,* "When Bradbury Press decided to publish Judy Blume's *Forever* . . . , they created an adult division, which they had never had before, probably hoping to forestall adverse criticism for presenting to teenagers a warm and positive story about premarital sex."[29] Richard Jackson explains, "Labeling it an adult book . . . was our way of saying that it didn't belong on children's shelves, that we were not recommending this for every fourth grader who'd just read her [Blume's] other books."[30]

At the time the book was written, the category "young adult" did not exist. "*Forever*," says Blume, "is a young adult book."

Teens and preteens are, of course, reading the book. If youngsters bring her copies of *Forever* to autograph, Blume asks how old they are. "If they say twelve, fine. But if they say nine, I say, 'Why don't you wait a few years,' or 'Make sure your parents read it too, and you can talk about it.' "[31] Among public libraries that own the book, it is shelved in both the adult and young adult sections. Trying to hide copies of *Forever* is like trying to hide Christmas presents. No matter where they are, the kids will find them.

Forever was the first of Blume's novels to find its way onto film. Blume had had several offers to film her other children's books, but, she says, "I felt less protective of *Forever* than *Margaret* or *Then Again* or *Blubber*." She was also impressed with the fact that one of the producers loved the story. Blume says, "She identified with the book completely and therefore did a good job with it." Blume also had enormous confidence in the ability of the director, John Korty, whom she calls "one of the best directors ever." She felt that he was "true to what the story was all about."

The movie was filmed in San Francisco, so that instead of going skiing, Michael and Katherine go rock-climbing. Blume felt that that did not alter the essence of the story. John Korty found the boy who plays Michael selling shoes in a store in Oakland, California. Katherine was played by Stephanie Zimbalist, who was nineteen at the time. "Overall," Blume says, "they had a very fine group of young actors without *names*. Some of them went on to do other things."

Scripts were written by several people, but Korty finally used dialogue directly from the book. The film was produced through EMI, and according to Blume, the producer at EMI fought long, hard battles with the CBS executives, who wanted to cut out the sex scenes. For the most part, the director won.

Reviewers in both the *Los Angeles Times* and the *New York Times* praised the film. John O'Connor in the *New York Times* says, "There are no true surprises in a film like 'Forever.' The story simply unfolds to its inevitable conclusion. But Mr. Korty's direction and an impressive collection of solid performances, particularly from Miss Zimbalist (daughter of Efrem Zimbalist, Jr.) managed to keep an oft-told tale absorbing. Perhaps that is surprise enough."[32] Said *Los Angeles Times* reviewer Kevin Thomas, "'Forever' is more than compassionate. It is honest and very true to its carefully established upper-middle-class milieu. Miss Zimbalist has not yielded to Butler right away, but when she does she visits a Planned Parenthood clinic in San Francisco not long afterward. What's more, her parents (Judy Brock, Tom Dahlgren) aren't ogres, but are rightly concerned."[33] Both reviewers applaud Mr. Korty's direction of the film.

Forever is a story about decision making. For Katherine, the decision to have sex with Michael is not impulsive. It is a story of real life, and for that reason, it is somewhat methodical. The important aspect of *Forever* is that it discusses life as it is in a format that kids will read. A major point that has been missed by critics who cannot get past "getting laid" is that relationships are more than sex, and that is an important message for kids to hear. Katherine is secure in the support she receives from her parents, from her grandmother, and even from her younger sister. Katherine's strength is grounded in generations of supportive family ties, and that, after all, is the basis for the love that lasts forever.

5

Making Deals with God

Are You There God? It's Me, Margaret. was a milestone, not only in Judy Blume's career, but in the history of literature for young people. *Margaret* (1970) was loaded with new words and new ideas. It was the beginning of a revolution. With very little sound and hardly any fury, *Margaret* ushered in the age of realism in fiction for young people; but Blume did not know when she wrote *Margaret* that she was being revolutionary. The book was merely a picture of a life she had known as a preteenager. Blume explains, *"Margaret* was the first book I wrote where I said 'O.K., now I write from my own experience,' and that's when I started to grow, as a writer and as a woman."[1] She says, further, "I didn't know enough to know I was being controversial."[2] Blume was a young wife and mother in her late twenties when she wrote *Margaret.* She had had two books published, *Iggie's House* for eight- to ten-year-olds and *The One in the Middle Is the Green Kangaroo* for the picture book set. Both had been mildly successful. What prompted Blume to write *Margaret?* In her words, "Writing for twelve-year-olds had a lot of appeal. When you're that age, everything is still out there in front of you. You have the opportunity to be almost anyone you want. I was not yet thirty when I started the book, but I felt my options were already gone."[3] Blume had been married almost ten years when she wrote *Margaret,* and her children were in school. She was an intelligent woman who thought her life was over. Perhaps in writing about a happier, albeit troublesome, time in her life, she could recapture the joy of her youth. She wrote as an escape from the suburban doldrums in which she found herself.

Richard Jackson tells the story of how *Margaret* came to be written: "Before *Iggie's House* was published, Judy was in my office one day, and she said, 'I've written most of another book. It's about a young girl who talks to God as if he's her friend. I don't know if you'll think it's any good.' From her description, it sounded terrific, and she sent it in and it became *Margaret*." Jackson goes on to say that the manuscript was unnamed as Blume delivered it, so a typist filled in the first line as its title, and it stuck. Jackson reveals that Blume is very fussy about the punctuation in the title. He says, "There is no comma before *God,* and there is a period after *Margaret.* There is no comma before *God* because Judy felt very strongly that there was no distance between Margaret and God, and she wanted it in this kind of informal, rushed way, the way people talk, the way people think." Later, Jackson says, when he and Blume discussed *Margaret,* "It was quite clear that Judy knew Margaret. She knew every one of those kids in that book from the gut out."

Starring Sally J. Freedman as Herself (1977) is also something of a milestone in Blume's career, but not in the same way *Margaret* is. *Sally* is notable in that it is the only one of Blume's books that is not set in the present. It is also the only one of her books for young people that is written in the third person. Blume has spoken of both *Sally* and *Margaret* as being closely autobiographical and has referred to both of them as her favorites. In an interview with Barbara Rollock, Blume said, *"Sally J. Freedman* is my most autobiographical book. I think it's the book I've been waiting to write. I had to get ready. In a way I feel all the other books were a rehearsal for this one."[4] When Blume says the book is autobiographical, she means that the family and the family situation are the closest of any of her books to her own childhood. The book is a harmonious blend of imagination and reality.

"Are you there God? It's me, Margaret. We're moving today. I'm so scared God. I've never lived anywhere but here. Suppose I hate my new school? Suppose everybody there hates me? Please help me God. Don't let New Jersey be too horrible. Thank you."

Margaret Ann Simon and her family have moved from their apartment in New York City to a house in New Jersey, but Margaret does not know why they have moved. When she asks, she is told that Farbrook, New Jersey, is close enough to New York City for her father to commute to his job and for her mother to have all the flowers and grass and trees she has always wanted. Margaret suspects that the real reason for leaving the city is to remove her from the influence of her grandmother, Sylvia Simon. Grandmother Simon is Jewish. She loves Margaret dearly and would be thrilled if Margaret decided to accept the Jewish faith. Sylvia Simon was not thrilled when her son married a Christian, but she learned to live with the marriage. Margaret's maternal grandparents take a dimmer view of the situation; thus, Margaret does not see them often.

Margaret has no trouble making friends in her new surroundings and is immediately invited to join a secret club, which the four members, after lengthy deliberation, name the PTS Club for Pre-Teen Sensations. Club members are not allowed to wear socks with their loafers and they each keep a Boy Book with a list of their favorite boys. Another rule is that they all must wear bras. Most important, "The first one to get her period had to tell the others about it. Especially how it feels." At their meetings, the girls spend a considerable amount of time discussing their bodies and what is—or is not—happening to them. At one PTS meeting, the girls compare their slowly developing shapes to those of models in a *Playboy* magazine that Margaret borrows from her father's night stand. They conclude this meeting with fifty "We Must Increase Our Bust" exercises.

Throughout the story, Margaret talks to God, making

deals to do work around the house and clear the dinner table every night if only he will help her grow "you know where." She asks him too for direction in choosing a religion, but most of all, if he could please see to it that she got her period, that would be great. As the story comes to an end, Margaret is stuffing her bra with cotton balls, and she has tried out various religions and chosen none. However, she does get her period and her final prayer is one of thanksgiving. "Thank you God. Thanks an awful lot . . ."

Sally's story is that of a ten-year-old Jewish girl spending a year in Miami Beach, Florida, at the end of World War II, with her mother, her grandmother Ma Fanny, and her brother, Douglas. The family has gone to Florida for the sake of Douglas's health, leaving their father, a dentist, in New Jersey to tend to his practice—events that are drawn from Blume's own life.

Sally begins at the end of World War II in 1945. The opening scene of the book is based on an incident in Judy's past. "I was in a rooming house in Bradley Beach, New Jersey, on the night the war ended, and I did get sick that night, and my mother was very angry with me, and I didn't understand her anger at the time."[5] Everyone else was joyfully celebrating the end of the war, thinking about relatives returning home from Europe, and it was not a convenient time for a child to be ill. Sally repeatedly tells her mother she does not feel well, but her mother tells her not to think about it, to "think about peace instead." Sally, unable to follow her mother's directions, throws up on the beach. "They went back to the rooming house and Mom took Sally's temperature. It was 103. She put Sally to bed, gave her some ginger ale to sip and lay a cold, wet washcloth on her forehead. 'If only I had listened when you first told me you weren't feeling well . . . I was so excited myself. . . .' "

The war has ended, but Sally imagines that old Mr. Zavodsky, a neighbor, is Hitler and that he is hiding out in Miami Beach. None of Blume's immediate family died in a concentration camp, but as a Jewish child Judy heard her parents and cousins discuss relatives in Europe who had gone "underground." Blume admits there was not a real Mr. Zavodsky in Miami Beach, but, she explains, "I think Sally has a great need for adventure, and of course she leads a very active fantasy life. Mr. Zavodsky answers Sally's need for mystery. Her great disappointment when Mr. Zavodsky dies is the loss of the game." In describing her feelings about the war, Blume says, "The war seemed to me from movies a very glamorous time that I had missed out on. I had great fantasies about being in the underground and saving the world."[6]

Although the mass death that resulted from the war was very real, the death that Sally (like Judy) is preoccupied with is the possible loss of her father. Sally prays that her father won't die. "Please God, let Doey-bird get through this bad year . . . this year of being forty-two . . . we need him, God . . . we love him . . . so don't let him die . . . Keep him well, God . . . you wouldn't let three brothers die at the same age, would you?"

Later in the story, Sally's father tells her that he too had worried that he would die at forty-two, like his brothers. Then he realized how foolish it was to worry about it. He goes on, "It's taught me something, though . . . I've learned what's really important . . . to experience everything that life has to offer . . . to be near the ones I love." Sally longs to be adventurous, as she perceives her father to be, but fears that she is more of a worrier, like her mother.

Sally is anxious, too, about the possibility that her brother Douglas will die. After all, it is for the sake of his health that they have come to Florida. Sally says, "If Douglas died it wouldn't be fun like when her aunts and uncles and Granny Freedman had died. After their funerals they'd sit shivah for a week, at Sally's house. . . . It seemed to Sally that somebody in her family was always dying."

"Sitting shivah" is, of course, a part of Jewish culture, and it was a very large part of Judy's life when she was growing up. She is quoted as saying, "A lot of my philosophy . . . came from growing up in a family that was always sitting shivah. . . . All my father's family died young, and he died when he was 54. I was surrounded by death. . . ."[7] Sally describes the fun of sitting shivah. "It was a Jewish custom, to help the family through those difficult first days following a loved one's death. Sally enjoyed sitting shivah very much. Every afternoon and evening friends and relatives would come to visit, bringing baskets of fruit and homemade cakes and cookies and boxes of candy from Barton's. And they would pinch Sally's cheeks, telling her how much she'd grown since the last funeral."

Neither *Sally* nor *Margaret* received rave reviews on publication. Jean Mercier's review of *Sally* in *Publishers Weekly* was the only review to which Blume has ever responded in writing. Mercier, who later apologized in person to Blume, described some parts of the book as "sickening," saying "Blume's approach will be resented as frivolous by many readers, since Sally's own relatives are victims of the Nazi death camps, not the stuff of humor. Neither are some other details in the book. In fact, parts are sickening."[8] When pressed by Blume to clarify what she meant, Mercier said that she had only intended to indicate that the one section in which a cockroach is found in the chow mein made her "lose her coffee." Because of Blume's close personal association with Sally's story, she was particularly hurt by the reviewer's comments.

In another scene that could indeed make one queasy, Sally imagines an encounter with Hitler in which he slashes each of her fingers with a knife and lets the blood drip on the floor. As the blood stains the carpet, Hitler cries, "Look what you've done, you Jew bastard, . . . you've ruined my rug!" *School Library Journal* reviewer, Diane Haas, commented regarding this scene that "Sally's obsession with Hitler, while certainly plausible and understandable, does not fit smoothly into the context of the book, and is often unnecessarily violent in its expression."[9]

This is a shocking scene, and one that would seem out of

context except for this particular Jewish child in this particular time and place. Sally is an extremely imaginative, dramatic child, who knows nothing of Hitler other than the bits and pieces she overhears from adult conversation. Blume explains, "What many adult readers have forgotten is that in 1947, adults didn't even know all of the horrors . . . But any child with imagination—which Sally had and which I had—made it up."[10]

Haas continues in a critical vein, "It seems almost painfully obvious that this is autobiographical, but in exorcising the demons of her youth, Blume is ignoring her eager audience and forgetting what she does best."[11] Blume told Barbara Rollock, "This book is very different. Please give me the freedom to be different. Don't ask me to do the same book again and again."[12] Blume was once told by an editor (not Richard Jackson) that she could be even more successful than she already is, by doing just this. But Blume is too creative to be able to adhere to a formula.

Perhaps what is troublesome to some adult reviewers is that Sally's story too closely resembles reality. In *Margaret* Blume is saying, "This is what it was like for us in sixth grade." In *Sally* she says, "This is what my life was *really* like." It is important to remember that the two books were written at very different times in Blume's life. *Margaret* was written when Blume was a young housewife with small children. The person who wrote *Sally* was not only seven years older, but also wiser and more reflective. Thus *Sally* is a slower-moving, more introspective story. *Sally* is the story of a young girl's relationship with her father—and with the rest of her family. Blume says that when her brother read the book, it made him much more aware of himself at that age and of his place within the family. *Margaret's* story, on the other hand, revolves around her relationships with her friends. We see her family only as part of the background.

Not all reactions to *Sally* were negative. One of the most favorable reviews appeared in the British publication the *Junior Bookshelf* when the book was published in England.

"The story moves at a good pace, with lively humour, in a mixture of narrative, Sally's stories, her correspondence with her father, and the letters (undelivered) to 'Hitler-in-disguise.' "[13] What is interesting is that Blume's British agent, when told about *Sally,* said, "I will never find anything about Hitler funny, and that book will never be published here." When, several years later, the book *was* published in England, Blume wrote a foreword explaining the story: "When World War II ended I was just seven years old, but the war had so coloured my life that it was hard to think of anything else. No one I knew had actually experienced the war first hand. . . . And yet I could not help worrying that it could happen again, could happen to us. I knew that Adolf Hitler was a menace. I knew that he wanted to kill all the Jews in the world. And I was a Jew."

Children's reactions to *Sally* have been mixed. According to Blume, "The children who love Sally are children like Sally. I get two kinds of letters about *Sally*—either 'Sally is such a weird kid' or 'I'm just like Sally.' When you are that kind of child, you're very careful not to let other people know."

Though low-key, the reaction to *Are You There God? It's Me, Margaret.* was much more enthusiastic, although the real fireworks did not go off for *Margaret* until the book was published in paperback in 1972. A paperback copy of *Margaret* cost seventy-five cents when it came out in that year, thus making it available to practically every youngster in the nation. This was the year of the paperback boom, and *New York Times Book Review* critic Margaret O'Connell stated: "May they continue to thrive. Paperbacks for children. There are now over 3,000 of them in print."[14] It was at that point that Blume learned who her true fans were—the children for whom she was writing.

Margaret was named a Best Book of the Year by the *New York Times,* and Dorothy Broderick's glowing review in that newspaper called it "a funny, warm and loving book, one that captures the essence of beginning adolescence."[15]

Publishers Weekly said, "Margaret's story is any young girl's story, but when Judy Blume writes it there is an exception—it is directed toward each reader individually."[16]

Jeannette Daane in *School Library Journal* was milder in her praise: "The writing is not as polished as in stories with similar contemporary suburban settings by Elaine Konigsburg, but the content is important, the dialogue (humorous and serious) is realistic and the feelings come through with sincerity."[17] When *Margaret* was published in England, the *London Times* reviewer was not impressed but thought that young readers would be. "The story is inconsequential. The book consists largely of the endless body-obsessed prattle of Margaret and her friends, and as such will prove irresistible to readers of her age."[18]

This type of review has become fairly common for Blume's books. Though it is not a unique reaction, it is still astounding to Blume. "What confuses me is most reviewers, even the negative ones, end up saying, 'But the children are going to love it.' This intrigues me. What do they mean? Are they condescending to the children? To me? Are they saying the books are rotten, but kids have no taste so it doesn't matter? I happen to think kids do have taste, and I write for them."[19]

Religion is a prevailing theme in both *Sally* and *Margaret.* As a child, Judy absorbed the culture of Judaism if not the religion. "I love family gatherings of any kind," she says. "I remember as a child going from New Jersey to my aunt's on New York's Upper West Side for the first night of Passover. She had a beautiful chaise longue in her bedroom, where they would put me down to sleep when we got there so I could get up later. But of course I wouldn't go to sleep because next to the chaise longue was a tiny glass table with delicate glass ornaments on it. What child could sleep in a setting like that?"

In an interview dealing with *Sally,* Blume told Barbara Rollock, "The Jewishness of Sally's family is cultural rather than religious. And this is very much the way I grew up. I grew up like Sally, not like Margaret."[20]

Sally does not talk about religion, but she displays a sense of morality on the first day of school when, guiltily, she takes off her socks and throws them into the trash basket in the restroom, "hoping that her mother would never find out. It was a terrible sin to throw away clothing when everyone knew the poor children in Europe were going half-naked. God could punish a person for throwing perfectly good socks away. She hoped he'd understand just this one time."

Like Margaret, Sally wants so very much to be like everyone else, and she knows God well enough to know that he is kind, perhaps fatherly—her father would understand the importance of not wearing socks when no one else was wearing socks.

Both Margaret's God and Sally's God are personal gods. Blume explains it in her own life: "Dressing up and going to Temple on the High Holy Days was very much a social thing. I never felt God in a synagogue, but I surely felt him when I was alone."

Margaret tries to find God in churches and synagogues, even going so far as attempting to confess her sins to a priest. Once in the confessional, Margaret loses her courage and later talks to God in the privacy of her own room: "I did an awful thing today . . . I picked on Laura Danker . . . I really hurt Laura's feelings . . . I've been looking for you God. I looked in Temple. I looked in church. And today, I looked for you when I wanted to confess. But you weren't there. I didn't feel you at all. Not the way I do when I talk to you at night. Why God? Why do I only feel you when I'm alone?" Blume says, "Religion to me has always been very, very, very personal, as you know from *Margaret.*"

Blume's father grew up as an Orthodox Jew. Her mother was also Jewish but was less conservative than her husband. "My father had a great deal of religion and that religion was important to him. He was such a philosopher anyway."

Blume recalls thinking, one year when her father did not go to Temple for Rosh Hashanah, that there had been too many tragedies, too many deaths, and he had lost his faith in God.

On a larger scale, Blume says, "What it means to be Jewish is that you have a history. Because people were Jewish at a given time in history—they died." When Blume visited Israel with her children, the most moving part of their trip was the visit to the Holocaust Museum. "I cried so hard, I don't even remember what I saw," she says.

This, then, is what *Sally J. Freedman* is about: Sally thinks about the deaths of millions of Jews in concentration camps and connects this in her mind to her fear in regard to her father's death. She therefore develops an intricate prayer ritual to keep her father safe but realizes she can do nothing to save the Jews who have been killed. They have, she realizes, died because of their religion, because they were Jewish. Blume talks about the religious rituals she developed as a child in Florida. "I had elaborate prayers that had to be said every day, so many times a day, in just the right way, or something bad would happen to my father."

Critics were not pleased with the treatment of the subject of religion in *Margaret*. Sheila Egoff gives us a variation on "the kids will like it anyway" theme: "The possible significance of religion in her [Margaret's] life is not confronted, nor need it be to satisfy readers."[21]

Philomena Hauck snipes, "The subject of religion does come up in one book. . . . This could have provided an opportunity to explore the possible significance of religion in the heroine's life. Instead, the issue is confined to some chats with God and a few visits to churches, where Margaret is more interested in the hats than the service."[22]

Agnes Perkins complains, "Either of her problems—religious ambiguity or fear that she will not develop normally—could be major concerns for a girl of her age, but their connection for the sake of humor is condescending and trivializes both of them."[23]

To surmise that Blume connects these two themes in order to be humorous is farfetched. The humor in the book does not stem from Margaret's talks with God regarding her development. Her talks with God are serious—they are serious to any twelve-year-old and they are serious to Blume. Juxtaposing two ideas—when will I have my period? what religion will I adopt?—strengthens the overall theme—I just want to be normal. Margaret says it all in this passage: "Life is getting worse every day. I'm going to be the only one who doesn't get it. I know it God. Just like I'm the only one without a religion. . . . Please . . . let me be like everybody else."

Blume thinks back to her own growing up years: "Everybody thinks they're not normal. You pretend, like everybody else, I'm normal. But inside you know you're not, the harder you try to be. And you're afraid to be yourself because there is no yourself. You don't even know who yourself is."

Who will be there to help kids through these terrible years? Fortunately, both Sally and Margaret have loving, understanding grandmothers. Sylvia Simon knits sweaters for Margaret with little tags in them that say, Made Especially for You by Grandma. She takes Margaret to cultural events at Lincoln Center and takes Margaret out for lunch afterwards. The image we have of Grandma Simon is warm and snuggly. She is the Jewish grandmother, with or without chicken soup. Even the most hardened critic cannot resist Grandma Simon. "Probably the most interesting female characterization is Sylvia, the fraternal grandmother who defies most stereotypes of 'aged' females. She is healthy, fun, apparently financially independent, active, dresses in contemporary fashion (even changes her hair color), takes cruises, vacations in Florida, brings delicatessen, and is very fond of Margaret," says Jon Shapiro and Geraldine Snyder in *Reading Horizons*.[24] By contrast, her Christian grandparents, whom we only meet once, are rigidly set in their ways, especially on the topic of religion. " 'Nonsense!' Grand-

mother said. 'A person doesn't choose religion.' 'A person's
born to it!' Grandfather boomed."

Sally's Ma Fanny is much like Margaret's Grandma Simon. Both Ma Fanny and Sally's mother are waiting for
Sally the first day she comes home from her new school in
Florida, but Sally turns to Ma Fanny for comfort. "Ma
Fanny put her arms around Sally and held her until she
stopped crying. Then she said, 'So that's the bad news,
mumeshana . . . now tell us the good news.' 'What good
news?' Sally asked. 'Something good must have happened
. . . you can't go a whole day without one good thing happening . . .' 'Well,' Sally said, sniffling, 'I met a girl named
Barbara. She seemed pretty nice.' "

Sally's father is nurturing, despite his absence in Sally's
life at this time. Sally tells her friend Andrea, "My father's
busy too but he always has time for me." Blume refers to
her own father as an "active" parent because he gave her
medicine and sat with her when she was ill and because he
did little things for her like clipping her toenails.

Sally's mom, on the other hand, is very tense. Her character is similar in some ways to Aunt Bitsy in *Tiger Eyes,*
especially when she warns Sally that she is not an experienced bicycle rider. Blume has commented that "Sally's
mother was very cautious, but she was not as cautious as
Judy's mother."

Yet as one critic points out, "Sally's mother shows her
love for Sally by telling her . . . she resembles Esther Williams—Sally's favorite actress. Later, she dabs her favorite
perfume on her daughter when Sally admires it."[25]

As Sally's father tells her when she says she wishes her
Mom was silly like he is, "She loves you . . . you know
that . . . not everybody can be silly." We see in this exchange Blume's struggle to accept her mother's personality,
so very different from her own.

Blume has said of *Sally,* "I think of it as a happy family
story." Sally's parents obviously love each other—Sally has
some trouble accepting and understanding this and some-

times feels excluded when they want to be alone after not having seen each other for several months. As Julia Whedon, in the *New York Times Book Review* points out, "The move to Florida, frightening for everyone, shows Sally what a family is all about. In particular, she confronts for the first time the mystery of her parents' connubial relationship. Witnessing their awkward, then tender, reunions, she feels the impact of their need for one another without fully understanding what it means."[26]

The character of Mrs. Simon in *Margaret* was denounced for stereotyped behavior by Jon Shapiro and Geraldine Snyder of the University of British Columbia. "Stereotypical female characterizations of emotionalism, dependence, passivity, conformity, etc., are recurring behaviors exhibited throughout the book."[27] She is guilty, according to Shapiro and Snyder, of an even more heinous crime. She is "nurturing in behavior." They go on to explain: "This is exemplified in actions such as purchasing items for Margaret, driving her places, and generally being there, seeing about dinner, and being sure Margaret gets to where her friends are."[28] The mother of Margaret's friend Nancy also comes under attack for being "one-dimensional." She "bowls on Mondays, plays bridge on Thursdays, and apparently helps organize carpools, even for Sunday School."[29] Shapiro and Snyder fail to mention that the first time Margaret meets Mrs. Wheeler she is "on the porch with her legs tucked under her and a book on her lap." This image indicates that Blume was thinking either consciously or subconsciously of her own mother, whom she says "was often curled up in a chair reading when I came home from school." Blume recalls a time when she herself became so absorbed in a book (*Them* by Joyce Carol Oates) that she forgot to make dinner for her family.

Shapiro and Snyder also attack the character of Margaret. "She is involved with a group of girls, concerned about school, what to wear for parties, becoming interested in boys, anticipating puberty, and worrying about not being like everybody else. She and Nancy tend to live a relatively affluent suburban life without much else but self as a source of concern."[30]

From the "protect the children" camp, we hear, "The physical signs of growing up dominate the minds of Margaret and her friends. This story . . . is a sad one, really. To an adult it seems a shame that the competitive jostle towards maturity should force itself into the child's consciousness at such an early age."[31]

Dorothy Broderick puts it all in perspective with this: "Margaret is a real preteen with stirrings of desire unencumbered by narrow-focused sex. That is to say, she is becoming aware of her own body without yet thinking of it in relationship to another's."[32]

Margaret is innocent to the point of naiveté in her beginning awareness of her body. She hides under the covers when she tells her mother she wants to wear a bra. Sally innocently asks her mother, "How about breasts . . . does it hurt when they start to grow?" "You shouldn't be thinking about breasts at your age," Mom says. Sally counters that some girls in her class already have them and that her friend Andrea, only a year older, wears a bra. Ma Fanny answers Sally's question: "They don't hurt, mumeshana . . . They grow quietly, when they're ready." Sally's mother changes the subject.

When Sally's Aunt Bette is expecting a baby and no one tells her what is happening, Sally finally asks her mother how a woman gets pregnant. Mom attempts to explain, then gives up and says she will have to find a book on the subject.

Margaret, who is in sixth grade, is told by her gym teacher that they will be studying "certain very private subjects just for girls" during the school year. Margaret's comment: "Why do they wait until sixth grade when you already know everything!"

As she does in most of her books, Blume touches on the subject of honesty in *Sally* and in *Margaret*. When they first arrive at their apartment in Florida, Sally thinks, "Why were they pretending? Why didn't one of them admit the truth. This place was a dump."

When Sally goes to school and is told by the nurse that she has headlice, her mother tells her, "Listen, honey . . . that nurse is crazy . . . she doesn't know what she's talking about. You don't have nits. And we'll never tell anyone about it, okay?"

In a scene that foreshadows *Tiger Eyes,* Sally's friend Barbara tells her that ever since her father's death, her mother gets drunk every Saturday night. "It would be better if she'd come out and tell us how she's feeling. . . ." "Grownups always keep things to themselves, don't they?" Sally says.

In *Margaret* the moment of truth comes when Margaret finds out her friend Nancy has lied about getting her period. Margaret is stunned. "I didn't know what to say. I mean, what can you say when you've just found out your friend's a liar! . . . I felt kind of sorry for Nancy then. I want my period too, but not enough to lie about it."

In 1965, before *Margaret* was published, Louise Figzhugh brought up the topic of menstruation in a fiction book for young people. *The Long Secret* (1965), however, does not present the positive feelings about menstruation that *Margaret* does. For example, when Harriet asks Janie, "What's it feel like?" Janie answers, "Yuuuuuchk . . . It has absolutely nothing to recommend it." She then goes on to explain what happens inside a woman's body when she has her period. These are the cold, hard facts, told with a scientific accuracy that Blume does not approach in *Margaret.*

Five years after *Margaret* Norma Fox Mazer treated the subject of menstruation in a novel for teens and preteens entitled *Saturday, the Twelfth of October* (Delacorte, 1975). It is a time-travel book in which Zan, the main character, journeys back to a prehistoric time when the coming of the menses was celebrated in ritual.

Sally may not be the rite-of-passage book *Margaret* is, yet Sally does make some changes during the year in Florida. She learns, or begins to learn, from her father about courage and about being adventurous. When she was preparing to leave for Florida, her father had told her, "This is going to be an adventure. . . ." "How do you know?" Sally asked. "Because every new experience is an adventure."

A symbol of the bravery she has gained is the ride in the Goodyear Blimp. Sally tries to match her brother's enthusiasm when her father mentions going for a ride, but the idea of it frightens her. She likes watching it, but riding in it is something else again. This scene is similar to one in *Tiger Eyes* in which the characters discuss taking a ride in a hot air balloon. Aunt Bitsy's reaction is similar to Sally's mom, who tells her husband emphatically, "I am *not* setting foot in that blimp."

Sally chooses adventure with her father rather than sitting on the ground and worrying with her mother. Later, in writing to her friend, Chrissy, Sally tells her, "I am in-between my mother and my father, not just about television, but about a lot of things." Sally learns that there are choices in life, and this time at least, she chooses adventure.

6

What Problems?

Then Again, Maybe I Won't (1971), more than any of Blume's other books, deals with the isolation of youth, and not coincidentally, with the isolation of old age. Lucy E. Waddey wrote in the *ALAN Review*, "Tony in *Then Again, Maybe I Won't* is cut off from his mother . . . , from his shoplifting neighbor, and from the friend he left behind in his old neighborhood. . . . In reality, adolescents feel isolated, alone, misunderstood by parents and friends."[1] Faith McNulty wrote in the *New Yorker*, "She writes about the loneliness of being young, about youthful secrets—fear, anxiety, longing, guilt. . . . Her kids are swept along by capricious currents. They struggle to keep their sense of humor, and to keep their heads above water."[2] That quite accurately describes the hero of *Then Again,* Tony Miglione.

Not only does Tony feel different, but *Then Again* is different from Blume's other books. It is her only book for this age group (eleven- to thirteen-year-olds) with a male protagonist. Tony's story also differs from other Blume stories in that it takes place in a working-class setting. When we first meet the Miglione family, it is living in a small house in Jersey City. Tony's father is an electrician; his mother works in the lingerie department of a large department store. His brother Ralph and his wife Angie live upstairs; Ralph is a teacher and Angie is going to school to get her teaching degree. Tony's maternal grandmother also lives with the family and does all the cooking—you can almost smell the veal parmagiana. Grandma cannot speak because of a cancer of the larynx, but she definitely communicates with, and is a part of, the family. One evening at dinner, Ralph announces that Angie is pregnant. This is not good news for the financially strapped household. However, everyone is supportive of the young couple, and they all agree that they will somehow survive. Mr. Miglione, without his family's knowledge, attempts to market a special type of electrical cartridge he has been working on in his basement workshop. He is successful and suddenly there is money. They move to the upper-middle-class suburb of Rosemont, taking with them nothing from their old life except Mr. Miglione's truck with his name painted on the door. That, too, eventually goes when a neighbor asks Tony if they are having work done on their house since she sees a truck in their driveway every day. With the new house comes a housekeeper, who insists on being in charge of the kitchen, and Grandma is ousted from what had been her domain. She has nothing left to do but sit in her room with the color television.

Tony is distraught over the changes in his family. His parents, he feels, are hypocritical; his new friends are dishonest; and his brother Ralph sells out to the system by quitting his teaching job and going to work for their dad. The stress of all this is too much for Tony, and he ends up in the hospital with acute stomach pains. When the doctors find nothing physically wrong with Tony, Dr. Fogel, a psychotherapist, listens with an understanding ear to Tony's problems. In time, Tony is able not only to understand but also to forgive his family, his friends, and himself.

The Council on Interracial Books for Children criticized Blume for choosing to make Tony's social-climbing family of Italian origin. "While the author shows that a rise in class status can mean a lowering of humanitarian impulses, one questions why the author chose a working-class family of Italian descent to make her point."[3] This criticism bothers Blume, who says the reason she wrote about an Italian family was that she has a close friend who is Italian and she was familiar with this woman's background and upbringing.[4] The fact that the family is Italian, other than for the sake of the descriptions of the grandmother's cooking, has no bearing on the story. The family could have been Scandinavian. It would not have altered the story. The point is that Blume is a novelist, and like any good writer, she takes incidents or objects or character traits from real life and weaves them into a story.

Richard Jackson says, "In *Then Again,* which I think is a vastly under-understood book, a kid is transplanted and doesn't have the chance to go back. And that transplanting is what that book is about. It's a class clash book. It's hard when your parents are upwardly mobile."

Once again, Blume uses moving to portray children's lack of control over their lives. But this time there is a twist. This young person moves not only to a new neighborhood but also to a new rung on the social ladder. Tony is not sure that is where he wants to be. He sees the good in having money: he is able to have spending money to buy some of the things he wants; he gets a new bike when he asks for it. But he also sees the disadvantages: his parents think they can fix whatever is wrong in the family by purchasing something. When Grandma retreats to her room, they buy her a TV set.

It is Tony's mother who spends most of her time climbing. (Blume is quick to point out that this character is *not* based on her own parent.) Tony's mother is like Deenie's in thinking that her child could not possibly have any difficulties—physical or mental. "What problems? A thirteen-year-old boy doesn't have any problems!" Blume was given somewhat the same message as a child—the perfect daughter would never have any troubles. Thus she kept a lot of her feelings to herself—and developed stomach pains and eczema.

Tony tells Dr. Fogel about his mother: "She's really a phony. . . . I'd love to tell her I think so." The reader gets the point that Tony is disillusioned not only with his mother but with most of the adults in his life. Tony also tells Dr. Fogel: "My father's really something. He's a good one! He just goes along with everything. Nothing bothers him." Mr. Miglione is a typical Judy Blume male parent, and like all her other calm, easygoing fathers, he speaks up when the time is right. When Frankie, Tony's friend from his old neighborhood, is coming to visit, Tony's mother says, "It's just that Jersey City is a long way off and you can't see each other very often so you might as well concentrate on your new friends." His father says, "There's no friend like an old friend! Right, Tony?" In the final pages of the story, when Mrs. Miglione thinks that perhaps Tony should go to a military school because his friend Joel is going, his father steps in with, "Let's leave the decision to Tony this time." A strong bond has formed between the father and son. Both have grown and changed and come to accept and respect each other.

Unfortunately, Mrs. Miglione does not change. But at least Tony can see some humor in his mother's thinking. "I almost laughed . . . 'If Mrs. Hoober told you Joel was going to the Juvenile Detention Center, would you ask me if I wanted to go too?' But I didn't say it. And I didn't get any pains either. Because it was funny. Funny and sad both." Tony's mother wants desperately to do the right thing in her new surroundings. She is pleased when Tony's father gets rid of his old truck and replaces it with a new car. "I'm glad you decided that way, Vic. We don't want to start off on the wrong foot here." When Tony tells his mother that maybe Grandma would come out of her room if his mother would let her do the cooking again, Mrs. Miglione replies, "How would that look to the neighbors . . . like she's the maid or something!"

Tony is sensitive enough to feel guilty about his grandmother. When his friend Frankie comes to visit and asks about her, Tony tells him, " 'She stays in her room most of the time. She . . . she doesn't feel too well.' I don't think I'll ever tell anyone the truth about Grandma. I'm too ashamed." As one reviewer observed, "[Tony] has guilt feelings about everything: his brother killed in Viet Nam, his grandmother whose place has been taken by the housekeeper, his friend Joel's shoplifting from posh stores and his splendidly amusing telephone pranks."[5]

Tony blames himself for the foolish way he sees his parents behaving. When Mrs. Hoober, the neighbor, calls Mrs. Miglione Carol, although her name is Carmella, Tony is furious at what he sees as his mother's hypocrisy. Mrs. Miglione is so anxious to please Mrs. Hoober and to make friends that she will do almost anything. When Tony's father comes to talk to him about it, Tony says, "I felt like I did on Veterans Day when I stood over Vinnie's grave . . . guilty!" On that day he had wondered, "Does Vinnie know about us now? . . . And if he knows, what does he think?" . . . Is he laughing and saying, 'Hey, what happened to you guys since you visited last year?' "

Tony does not feel the same deep sadness his mother feels over his brother's death; thus he feels guilty for surviving and for being able to go on with his life when his mother feels so miserable. Mrs. Miglione does nothing to include Tony, or anyone else in the family, in her grieving. En route to the cemetery, Tony tells us, "My mother sniffled and I knew what was coming. Every year she devotes the whole day to talking and crying and saying *if only* about Vinnie. I always feel like an outsider on Veterans Day."

Tony and Grandma are both outsiders. They are both dependent on others in the family for their livelihood. Neither is consulted when it came to moving the family to a new home. They simply are moved. Grandma is allowed to bring along her old pots and pans, but she never uses them. The old pots and pans do not belong in the new kitchen and thus Grandma does not belong. From the beginning, Grandma is skeptical of this new work space. She spends the first few days in Rosemont in the kitchen. "She opened every cabinet a million times and wrote my mother a whole pad full of notes. . . . My mother kept telling Grandma what a wonderful kitchen it is . . . so modern! . . . My grandmother kept shaking her head."

As outsiders, Tony and Grandma have no one to cling to

but each other. Therefore when Tony realizes he cannot communicate with his parents, that his friend Joel is a shoplifter, and that his brother Ralph is quitting a job he loved in order to make more money, he turns to Grandma. "I stood there for a while, thinking that me and Grandma have a lot in common. We're both outsiders in our own home. I knocked on the door and called, 'Grandma.' When Grandma opened it and saw me she turned off her TV. Then she sat down in her chair and held her hands out to me. I went to her and I started to cry." Grandma comforts Tony. Without saying a word, the two of them are able to express their deepest feelings. This is a powerful, climactic scene. Blume has said of her own grandmother, who lived with her family in Florida, that if no one else loved you, Grandma always did.

In striving to give their son everything he wants—a new bike, binoculars, a basketball hoop—the Migliones have neglected to give him a part of themselves. Blume sees this pattern over and over again in the letters she gets from young readers. "Most of all, kids today seem to want what people always want—to be loved and accepted."[6] Any warmth that may have been present in the Miglione home in Jersey City turned to ice when they moved to Rosemont. In the old house there was the real warmth of Grandma's cooking. Like a spaghetti commercial, Tony comes home from school and asks what's for supper. In the new house with its modern kitchen, the servant, Maxine, not only does the cooking but stands over them while they eat waiting for Tony's father to compliment the food. Grandma, meanwhile, is in her room; she does not join the family for meals. The last sign of affection readers see between the parents is prior to their move. "When Mr. Miglione returns with the news of their success, his wife calls him a genius and gives him a 'juicy kiss.' "[7]

The only communication between Tony and his father after the move is an occasional game of chess, and one short discussion about sex. The talk is brief, since Tony's father determines that Tony knows what he needs to know and has the right information. Just to be safe, however, the next day he hands him a book called *Basic Facts About Sex*. Julia Kagan in a *McCall's* article entitled "What They Really Want to Know," points out, "As is true of all Judy Blume versions of this scene, the parent ends the talk by giving his child a book. . . . 'Using a book is not a cop-out,' says Blume. . . . 'It shows that the parent may not know or be comfortable telling the child all the answers— . . . but the parent is willing to help him find out what he wants to know.' "[8]

At the old house, there was at least a semblance of humor, in Tony's jokes. When Ralph announces Angie's pregnancy and everyone at the table becomes very quiet, Tony tries to laugh and says, "What's everybody so gloomy about? They're married!" In Rosemont there is not much to laugh about, but by the end of the story Tony is beginning to regain his sense of humor.

In addition to the humor, the Migliones also leave behind their friends and their furnishings when they leave Jersey City. The one thing Tony wants to take along is his Jefferson Junior High wall pennant. His mother objects. "It's old," she says. "What do you need it for?" As they are leaving, Tony gives the pennant to his friend Frankie, thereby saying goodbye to the last reminder of his old neighborhood.

Tony tries to make friends in his new neighborhood, but it is not easy when the one kid Tony wants to know better is a chronic shoplifter. Joel Hoober cannot walk into a store without picking up something and stuffing it into his pockets. When Joel is finally caught shoplifting and his father decides to send him to a military academy, Joel tells Tony, "That's how George Hoober deals with his problems. He puts them away some place." Tony learns to deal with his problems in a way that Joel's father does not.

The book was well received by reviewers. But more important for Blume was a comment from an eleven-year-old fan who said, "I thought *Maybe I Won't* was neat. It was about a boy who wants to be a friend, but doesn't know how. I can't make friends that easy, either. It made me feel better that other people have the same trouble.'"[9]

Tony will survive. Grandma probably will, too. As for the rest of the Miglione family, maybe they will—then again, maybe they won't.

At two and a half: "Wearing this bathing suit is one of my earliest memories."

about three, with brother David, out seven.

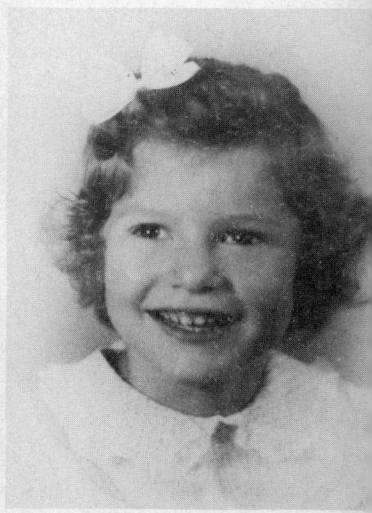

At about five.

"The Sally J. Freedman Years," in Miami Beach, aged nine and ten:

Sally J. Freedman in ballet clothes.

Judy's parents, Esther and Rudolph Sussman.

At nine.

On the beach with
brother David.

Bunk photo at Camp Kenwood, 1952. Judy, fourteen, is in the first row on the far right.

"Sweet Sixteen."

With Larry, three, and Randy, five, in 1966, at Randy's graduation from nursery school.

Answering fan mail, Santa Fe.

With Randy and Larry, Santa Fe.

Summer on Martha's Vineyard.

With favorite uncle, Bernie Rosenfeld, and mother, Esther Sussman, at New York University award ceremony.

George and Judy, 6 June 1987: "Our very informal wedding on the terrace in New York."

Just As Long As It's Not the End of the World

Though written years apart, *It's Not the End of the World* (1972) and *Just As Long As We're Together* (1987) are cut from the same bolt. Woven throughout both stories is the dilemma parents face in attempting to discuss their own problems with their offspring. For the Newmans and the Hirsches the problem is divorce. But how do you tell the children? Awkwardly or not at all is the answer in both cases. Blume believes in telling children the truth. When parents withhold information, perhaps out of fear, there are inevitable repercussions within the family.

It's Not the End of the World was not an easy book for Blume to write. In order to create the story, she did "considerable reading and six months of crying." At the time Blume wrote the book she had not personally experienced divorce but knew a number of families who had. She says, in *Letters to Judy,* "When my children were young we lived in a suburban New Jersey neighborhood, and as family after family split up my kids became fearful that this could happen to us, too. I tried to reassure them but I wasn't really sure myself. I wrote *It's Not the End of the World* at that time, to try to answer some of my children's questions about divorce, to let other kids know they were not alone and, perhaps, because I was not happy in my marriage. I kept those feelings deep inside. For years I would not, could not, admit that we had any problems. The perfect daughter had become the perfect wife and mother."[1] Since that time, she has undergone divorce herself, and while, she says "it wasn't easy, it wasn't the end of the world for any of us."[2]

Honesty is a theme that plays a part in all of Blume's writing. In *It's Not the End,* it steals the show. Blume says, "It's knowing that something is going on but not knowing what; it's that adult secretiveness that makes life so difficult for kids."[3] Richard Jackson concurs: "To me, *It's Not the End of the World* is about honesty as a kid experiences it, rather than divorce."[4] Blume admits that she had a difficult time being honest with herself, with her children, and with a family counselor following her divorce.

It's Not the End of the World is the story of Karen Newman, who is in sixth grade, her older brother Jeff, and her younger sister Amy. Karen says, with immediate honesty, "Then there are my parents. They're always fighting." She confirms her suspicions that something is decidedly wrong when her father leaves the house after an argument with her mother and is not home the next morning. Like Tony in *Then Again,* when no one tells her what is happening, Karen makes it up. When her Aunt Ruth says that her father is not home Sunday morning because he has "some business to take care of," Karen theorizes that he must be selling the store. She tells herself that her mother is upset because now they won't have as much money as before.

When Aunt Ruth, Uncle Dan, and Karen's mother take the children to a restaurant for lunch to announce the Newmans' divorce, the scene is an outright disaster. Karen jumps up, leaves the table, and runs outside. Her aunt follows and her mother brings her an ice cream cone. As in *Tiger Eyes* the adults try to cover an emotional situation with food. Later, Karen's younger sibling, Amy, begins having dreams that her entire family is going to disappear, and Karen's brother, Jeff, acts out his anger with his parents by running away. Meanwhile, Karen is trying frantically to bring her parents back together. By the end of the story, Karen has come to grips with the inevitability of her parents' divorce, her brother has returned home, and her little sister is telling silly jokes again. It is not exactly a happy ending, but it is not the end of the world.

Divorce is not an easy subject to discuss with a child as there is never just one reason for the collapse of a relationship. The difficulty is illustrated when Karen follows her mother to her bedroom after she returns from visiting her attorney in an attempt to draw an honest answer from her concerning the divorce. Karen is persistent in her questioning, and eventually her mother sits down next to her on the bed, takes her hand, and reassures her that both parents love all three of their children. This is helpful, to a degree, but Karen is searching for facts, for solid information. She tries talking to her older brother but finds that it is not easy getting through to him either. Karen says, "Trying to get to talk to Jeff is like banging your head against the wall. You just don't get anywhere. I've been tagging along after him for three days now but he says he's very busy and I should get lost."

Uncle Dan provides Karen with some of the hard data about divorce: legal aspects, custody, and child support. Like Deenie being fitted for her Milwaukee brace, Karen feels more secure knowing the details of what is happening in her life.

Just as Karen is beginning to despair of ever finding out anything about divorce, she meets Val Lewis. Val is the same age as Karen, but she is in seventh grade and her parents are divorced. Val knows all there is to know about divorce because she has purchased for herself *The Boys and Girls Book About Divorce* for $7.95. She read about it in the *New York Times,* she tells Karen.

Though Val is not a major character, she is significant in that she provides Karen with the information that eventually helps her accept the reality of her parents' divorce. Despite the fact that her appearance in the book is short-lived, Val is an extremely vital and well-drawn character. Blume makes Val come alive with details about her physical characteristics ("She has long black hair and bangs that cover her eyebrows. Her eyes remind me of Mew's.") and about her room ("She had a big desk with lots of drawers, plus a rug on the floor shaped like a foot, with toes and everything.") In addition, Val says, when Karen asks her how she knows so much, "I told you, . . . I read the entire *New York Times* every Sunday." That line reminds the reader of Blume's love for New York City, and also says that kids are certainly as smart as, if not smarter than, many adults.

Blume is, however, not unkind to parents. She does not present the Newmans as uncaring people or, for that matter, as no-good parents. They are so inevitably caught up in themselves and their emotions that they are incapable of sharing their anxieties with their children.

The highly charged climax of the book occurs when Karen begins screaming hysterically during one of her parents' heated arguments. Karen's father slaps her and she cries. The next day he calls to apologize. Her mother apologizes, too.

Despite the fact that both parents tell Karen they did not mean the things they said during the argument, Karen now sees that, in truth, her parents' marriage is over. She says, "Now I know the truth. My parents are not going to get back together. And there isn't one single thing I can do about it! My mother doesn't think Daddy is a wonderful person. She was feeding me a bunch of lies. Val was right. Not that Daddy thinks much of Mom either. Well, I'm through fooling myself." If no one else will be honest with Karen, at least she will be honest with herself.

Would there have been an easier way for Karen to learn that adults do not always tell the truth? Perhaps. But it was necessary for Karen to arrive at this realization herself in order for her to change and grow as a character. It is a difficult but necessary lesson. She finds out that adults are not always truthful, they are not always open with their feelings, and they are not infallible.

Another adult with imperfections is Karen's sixth-grade teacher, Mrs. Singer. Karen describes her in the opening

lines of the book. "Just look at Mrs. Singer. Last year she
was Miss Pace and everybody loved her. I said I'd absolutely die if I didn't get her for sixth grade. But I did—and
what happened? She got married over the summer and now
she's a witch!" Mrs. Singer sprays her hair with hair spray
in front of the class and lectures them about good manners.
For all this, however, Mrs. Singer is kindhearted. When
Karen asks to bring home her Viking diorama from the
display case, in hopes that it will help bring her parents
together, Mrs. Singer quietly takes the project out of the
showcase and gives it to her. Karen is so wrapped up in her
own problems by this point that she fails to thank Mrs.
Singer. Her only comment is, "I guess even witches have
good days!" Despite her self-centeredness, Karen reaches
out to help her younger sister Amy. Amy comes into
Karen's room in the middle of the night because she is
afraid and Karen comforts her until she falls asleep. But
Karen is wide awake, wishing she had someone to talk to.
She thinks about her friend Debbie and about how much it
would help if she could tell Debbie the truth about her parents. She also thinks about how Debbie always makes her
laugh. "She'll be able to cheer me up. Besides making monkey faces, Debbie has a very good sense of humor."

With Blume, there is always humor, despite the serious-
ness of the subject. As Myra and David Sadker describe *It's
Not the End of the World* in their textbook on children's
literature, "The situation presented is poignant but relieved
by some very funny moments." They go on to compare *It's
Not the End* to Peggy Mann's *My Dad Lives in a Downtown
Hotel* (1973) but say, correctly, that the Mann book, "is a
sadder book, one without Judy Blume's touches of humor to
provide relief."[5] *It's Not the End of the World,* in fact, ends
on a note of humor. Karen has told her friend Debbie that
she might be moving away, and she comes over to present
Karen with a going-away gift. "Debbie reached into her
skirt pocket and pulled out two pictures . . . I looked at
them. They were of Debbie making monkey faces." Finally,

Amy's riddles had always been a source of amusement for the family. She tells one early in the story, but the fun stops when all the quarreling begins. In the final scene, Amy is telling riddles again. Karen laughs. Everything will be all right.

Dick Jackson talks about a morality that exists in many of Blume's books—the loving, caring tenderness of an older sibling toward a younger brother or sister. It is present in *It's Not the End of the World* when Karen comforts Amy; it appears in *Tiger Eyes* when Davey calms Jason's fears that his mother will also die.

In *Just As Long As We're Together* another sweet younger sibling in need of solace appears. Stephanie Hirsch has a ten-year-old brother who has nightmares about nuclear war. One night when he has a nightmare and Mrs. Hirsch is not home, Stephanie goes in to comfort him. "I sat down at the edge of his bed. He threw his arms around me, sobbing. I held him tight. I would never put my arms around him during the day. Not that he'd let me. His face felt hot and wet with tears. He smelled like a puppy."

Later, Stephanie assuages Bruce's fears regarding their parents' separation. For his sake she talks optimistically about the possibility that their parents will get back together. As she returns to her room, she says, "I got into bed feeling a lot better. It's funny how when you try to help somebody else feel better you wind up feeling better yourself."

Stephanie's ten-year-old brother is an antinuclear activist, but Blume is quick to point out that "nobody asked me to put him there." Bruce is an integral part of the story, and he also serves to tell us something about Blume's deep-seated moral convictions. She says, "I think war is stupid, just like Bruce does in my book. It's stupid that we can't come up with an alternative."

Along with the care and concern of one child for another, *Just As Long* displays elements that Blume has used in other stories. Like *Deenie* it is a story about three friends; like *Are*

You There God? it deals with menstruation; and like *It's Not the End of the World* it deals with divorce. In *Just As Long,* as in most of Blume's stories, someone has recently moved.

The theme of moving emerges repeatedly in Blume's books. First, in *Iggie's House* Winnie's friend Iggie has moved and a new family, who happens to be black, moves into Iggie's house. Next, we meet Margaret in *Are You There God? It's Me, Margaret.,* and she is busy making new friends in her new neighborhood in Farbrook, New Jersey. Tony's family in *Then Again, Maybe I Won't* moves because of its new economic status. Sheila in *Sheila the Great* moves for the summer, and Sally in *Sally J. Freedman* moves to Miami for a year. Peter Hatcher's family, in *Superfudge,* moves to Princeton so that his father can write a book on "the history of advertising and its effect on the American people." In *Tiger Eyes* Davey and her mother and brother leave the home that was the site of her father's killing and flee to the perceived safety of Los Alamos. In *Just As Long* Stephanie says, "We moved over the summer and for weeks our new house reeked of paint." Unlike some of Blume's other characters, Stephanie is pleased with the move, since she is now closer to her best friend, Rachel.

Rachel is a perfectionist. She has her books arranged alphabetically on her shelves, and the hangers in her closet all face the same way. Enter Alison, new kid on the block. Alison may be new, but she does not exhibit the typical insecurities of a new kid. The first day of junior high Stephanie describes Alison waiting at the bus stop. "Alison was wearing baggy pants, a white shirt about ten sizes too big, and running shoes. She had sunglasses around her neck, on a leash, and a canvas bag slung over her shoulder. The tangles were brushed out of her hair but her part was still crooked. All in all she looked great." Alison is adopted—she's Vietnamese—and her mother is a well-known television actress.

Blume offers a peek into her own life when Stephanie asks Alison what it's like having a mother who is famous. Alison replies, "It doesn't matter that she's famous. . . . When she's home, she's Mom." Blume's daughter Randy had a similar conversation with friends.

It is easier for Stephanie's mother in *Just As Long* to face the possibility of a divorce than it is for Karen's mother in *It's Not the End* since Stephanie's mother operates her own travel agency. There are no screaming fight scenes in *Just As Long*. The Hirsches are more calm and matter-of-fact about their separation than the Newmans, perhaps partly because of Mrs. Hirsch's financial independence. Blume realizes that confronting a divorce without an economic cushion is not easy. She says, in *Letters to Judy*, "I know, from the letters I have received, that divorce for women who have no means of support, except the checks that their ex-husbands may or may not send regularly, and which may not even be enough to feed and clothe the children, let alone pay the rent, is a very different kind of nightmare for a family."[6]

In *Just As Long* all the mothers—and grandmothers—work. Stephanie's grandmother is a stockbroker in New York. The mother of Stephanie's friend Rachel is a trial lawyer. Stephanie says, "Mrs. Robinson is always either starting a big case or in the middle of one." The best friend from college of Stephanie's mother "has a very good job. She produces a news show for NBC." Stephanie tells us, in an aside, "Carla is a widow. Her husband was killed while he was crossing the street."

The relationship between Stephanie and Rachel changes as Stephanie becomes best friends with Alison, too. Meanwhile, Stephanie's parents have separated without telling either of the children. Like Karen in *It's Not the End*, Stephanie does not tell her friends about her family's problems, and she also tries briefly to get her parents back together.

Stephanie is angry with both her parents and she acts out her anger by overeating. Soon her classmates are calling her El Chunko. We see Stephanie attacking the leftovers from Thanksgiving dinner after she has learned about her parents' separation. As Jane Resh Thomas, noted author and children's book reviewer for the *Minneapolis Star Tribune,* states, "The feelings and responses are as authentic as anger toward separated parents, and overeating to assuage it."[7]

To make matters worse, Stephanie has an argument with Rachel about her parents. Rachel brings it out in the open that she knows about Stephanie's parents and accuses Stephanie of being a liar for not sharing the information with her friends.

By the end of the story Stephanie and Rachel reconcile their differences, and there is a possibility that Stephanie's parents will reconcile theirs. Josephine Humphreys of the *New York Times Book Review* finds the ending unsettling. "Although hope is surely not one of the dangers that children should be protected from, to offer *this* hope, here, is hardly consistent with the honest realism for which Judy Blume is known."[8] Nevertheless, the upbeat ending is appropriate to this story. Blume does not believe in "happily ever after," but we know that the characters will be able to resolve their problems because they have shown their strength. Stephanie has taken charge of her life by deciding to control her weight; Stephanie's mother is in control of her life, fiscally and emotionally; and Stephanie's father has broken up with his girlfriend and is moving back to New York.

Just As Long As We're Together does not have the emotional peaks and valleys of *It's Not the End of the World.* In both books, however, the main characters find their way out of their problems: Karen through her sense of humor and Stephanie by regaining her sense of optimism. Both Karen and Stephanie would agree that no matter what happens to them or to their families, "It's not the end of the world."

8

The Merry Books

When Judy Blume decided she wanted to write books for children, she went to the library and checked out stacks of children's books. "I loved Beverly Cleary's books," she recalls. "I fell off the couch laughing. I knew I wanted to write books like those." And she has. Like Cleary's books, Blume's *Tales of a Fourth Grade Nothing* (1972), *Otherwise Known as Sheila the Great* (1972), *Superfudge* (1980), and *Fudge-a-mania* (1990) are based on bizarre, often humorous, real-life incidents and are written for children roughly eight to twelve years of age. Richard Jackson, although not the editor of these titles, has aptly named the four "The Merry Books."

The character of Fudge, for example, in *Tales* and *Superfudge* is based on Blume's son Larry when he was small. Blume says that Larry never actually refused to eat as Fudge did but enjoyed a meal or two under the dining-room table, calling himself Frisky the Cat. She goes on, "He once spread mashed potatoes on the wall of a Howard Johnson's Restaurant and gleefully dumped a bowl of peas on his head. He did suck four fingers on his left hand and made the same slurping noise that Fudge makes in the book, and there was that Thanksgiving when he refused to wear his new red shoes and, after much kicking and screaming, we took him out to dinner in just his socks."[1] When *Tales of a Fourth Grade Nothing* was published, *Booklist* lamented that the character of Fudge was "too exaggerated to be very believable."[2]

The summer Blume spent bicycling around Southwest Harbor, Maine, provided the setting for *Fudge-a-mania*. Because she spent so much time peddling, she found herself a frequent visitor at Bicycle Bob's, and he became a character in the story. In the book, Bicycle Bob welcomes Peter into the I.S.A.F. (I Swallowed a Fly) Club. Bob suggests that the only cure for swallowing a fly is an ice cream cone from Ickle's. In real life, Blume's son Larry rides his ten-speed all over New York City. The first time he swallowed a fly while biking he called his mother and reported the incident. When *Fudge-a-mania* was completed, Blume told Larry she had invented the I.S.A.F. Club just for him. He blithely replied, "Oh, I must have swallowed half a dozen by now."

Blume is a master at pulling humor out of a predicament that others might find devastating. She says, "Most children think my books are funny and that pleases me, because humor is so often the only way to get through a difficult situation. Humor can bring people closer together. I can't set out to be funny in my books; it has to happen by itself. It has to grow out of a situation."[3]

Many of the incidents in *Tales, Sheila, Superfudge,* and *Fudge-a-mania* are funny. Ask any ten-year-olds or their teachers. A fourth-grade teacher says, "*Superfudge* and *Tales of a Fourth Grade Nothing* are among their favorites— all the things they're feeling are the things the characters feel . . . after I've read a book like *Superfudge* that makes them all laugh out loud, these kids will go and get that book and look up the funny parts."[4] A scene in *Tales* that youngsters relish is the moment when Mr. Hatcher picks up a bowl of cereal that Fudge refuses to eat and dumps it over the child's head. Younger children appreciate the slapstick humor of the incident, while older children identify with Peter and snicker when he says, "For once my brother got what he deserved. And I was glad!" When the Seattle Children's Theatre adapted *Tales* for presentation in the spring of 1987, loud whispers of "eat it or wear it" could be heard throughout the theater before every performance.[5]

Another technique that Blume uses to instill humor in her writing is the literalness of young children. In *Fudge-a-*

mania, Peter tells Fudge, "Fine. . . . You want to cook your own goose . . . go ahead." Fudge laughs and answers, "I don't have a goose, Pete." Eight- to twelve-year-olds appreciate the humor in this exchange because they understand the joke.

Tales, Sheila, Superfudge, and *Fudge-a-mania* are the most humorous of any of Blume's work, yet they portray the pathos—in the form of the fears, frustration, insecurity, and powerlessness of youth—that is present in most of her writing. In fact, without the anguish, there would be no humor. Beverly Cleary quotes James Thurber as saying, "Humor . . . lies closest to . . . that part of the familiar which is humiliating, distressing, even tragic."[6]

Tales of a Fourth Grade Nothing actually began as a picture book entitled *Peter, Fudge, and Dribble.* It was rejected by several editors before Ann Durell at Dutton suggested that Blume turn the story into a longer book using the same characters. One editor who rejected the book gave as an explanation that "it could never happen in real life." In fact, the idea for the story came from a newspaper account of a little boy who swallowed a turtle. Blume liked Durell's suggestion. "The idea appealed to me very much, and I went home and spent the summer writing about the Hatchers. I had a lot of fun, and as the book grew so did the characters, until they were all my special friends."[7]

The character of Peter Hatcher is what makes *Tales of a Fourth Grade Nothing, Superfudge,* and *Fudge-a-mania* universally enjoyable. Readers can identify with Peter's feelings of insecurity as, in *Tales,* he wins Dribble, the turtle, as first prize but secretly wishes he had gotten a goldfish like everybody else. When he sees all the other kids looking at his turtle and knows they are wishing they had gotten one too, he changes his mind. On the one hand, Peter enjoys being the envy of all the other kids; on the other hand, he does not want to be different. Like several other Blume characters, he just wants to be normal.

Nor is it difficult to identify with Peter's frustration in

Tales when he receives the *Big Picture Dictionary* from Mrs. Yarby, the wife of one of his father's clients. He thanks her politely, while thinking that a *good* book would have been a swell present but a big picture dictionary is for babies. In fact, he already has the book.

Sheila, a minor character in *Tales,* appears in her own book, *Otherwise Known as Sheila the Great,* where she divulges her greatest and most secret fears. Sheila is deathly afraid of Peter Hatcher's dog, Turtle, and she is afraid of water and learning to swim. She is afraid of noises in the dark and has a terrible time sleeping the first night in the family's summer house.

Blume admits to her own share of childhood fears, including attics, thunderstorms, and a particular stained-glass window. She says, "When I was little, I was terrified of a stained-glass window in a church that we often drove past. My mother would warn me so I could hide under the dashboard and not see the 'lady without the face.'" Blume has come to grips with most of these fears, although she admits to heading for a closet when she hears a thunderstorm approaching.

Like Sheila, Blume learned to swim with one foot on the bottom of the pool. Blume now enjoys several water sports, including sailing, canoeing, and kayaking. She and her husband set out in the summer of 1990 to kayak in every pond on Martha's Vineyard. Blume agreed to take sailing lessons when she met Cooper. "I was so in love," she says, "I would have sailed the entire Atlantic coast singlehandedly." Cooper had sailed all his life. But Blume became a sailing school dropout. "I had to drop out," she explains. "I knew I would be the only person not to get a diploma."

Blume says about Sheila, "I was surprised when I started getting letters about her. After all, she has a fairly small part in *Tales.* But kids wanted to know more about her." And Blume realized during the filming of *Otherwise Known as Sheila the Great* in 1988 that she wanted to know more about her too. Blume says, "I loved writing about Sheila again in *Fudge-a-mania*. There is something about her I really enjoy. She just keeps going, no matter how bad it gets." Linda Johnson, reviewing for *Library Journal,* doesn't seem to care if she ever finds out anything more about Sheila. "Due to Blume's vague characterization of her heroine, readers will wonder if 'Sheila the Great' is a fearful, insecure child . . . , a spoiled brat who lies constantly, or is simply a normal young girl with typical growing pains."[8]

Blume defends Sheila, saying, "Sheila's really hiding her fears, and I don't see her as a nasty child at all."[9] Sheila is portrayed as neither a spoiled brat nor a chronic liar. She is a typical child who is afraid to admit that she is afraid and who lies to cover her fears. Sheila tells Marty, her swimming instructor, that "the reason I cannot possibly put my face in the water of this pool is that I am scared!" He tells her how proud he is of her. "Do you realize that this is the first time you've been honest with me?" Marty asked. "You've finally admitted it . . . you're scared." *Publishers Weekly* picked up on this angle saying, "Sheila is faced with situations that demand honesty and the overcoming of her problems."[10]

Sheila's parents are extremely patient in dealing with Sheila's phobias. They insist she take swimming lessons although they know she is afraid and hint that they might get a dog because Sheila's sister, Libby, wants one. Sheila's parents never trivialize her fears but are firm and loving in dealing with them. When Sheila thinks of one excuse after another to escape going to her swimming lesson, her mother is one jump ahead of her. "I told her that I forgot my bathing cap so I wouldn't be able to put my head in the water. But she pulled out a new cap and said she brought one along just in case. And then she delivered me to Marty."

Superfudge revisits the Hatcher family, but they have moved. Peter complains to his parents when they tell him they have already rented a house in Princeton, "You should have told me before. Just like you should have told me about Tootsie as soon as you knew. You never tell me anything." Peter stalks off to his room, and later, when his mother comes to talk to him, she mentions that Fudge will be in kindergarten at the same school where Peter will be in sixth grade. Peter is outraged when his mother suggests he might enjoy a new experience. "You think it's fun to go to a new school? I don't even know anybody there."

Peter survives the year in Princeton, and at the end of the story his parents involve him—and Fudge—and baby Tootsie in the decision of whether or not to return to "Nu Yuck." Blume declares her own love of New York City when Peter says, "So, we're going back, I thought. Back to the Big Apple. . . . To some people there's no place like Nu Yuck. And I guess I'm one of them!"

The Hatchers are understanding of their offsprings' actions. As Susan Smith, in a graduate paper on parents in Blume novels, comments, "Even when Fudge is at his most trying, his parents maintain their loving, warm behavior. In the midst of her anger at Fudge for papering his sister with trading stamps (*Superfudge*), Mrs. Hatcher tells her exasperating child that she loves him."[11] Fudge asks his mother, "Don't you love your little boy?" He knows that she does, but at this point he could use some reassurance.

A theme that runs through many of Blume's books could be called family ties. Both the Hatchers and the Tubmans show genuine respect for their partners. They love their children, and the siblings in turn display consideration for each other. In *Superfudge* Peter holds Tootsie, carries her, and puts her in her car seat. Despite his frustrations with Fudge, when, in *Superfudge*, Peter thinks his brother might have been hurt, he feels genuine sadness. *"This is it, I thought. It's all over. They've found him, splattered across the road, his bike a mangled mess . . . I felt a big lump in my throat. If only I'd let him come on the picnic with me, none of this would have happened."* In *Fudge-a-mania*, when Fudge's myna bird, Uncle Feather, is lost, Peter treks through the fog with his brother searching for it.

We see this same kindness toward siblings in other Blume books. In *Deenie* her sister gives her clothes when Deenie has trouble finding something that will fit over her brace. We see an older sister caring about a younger brother in both *Tiger Eyes* and *Just As Long As We're Together*. In *Forever* the parents are respectful of their children, especially of their privacy. A realistic aspect of family life is shown in *Superfudge* by Fudge's interest in his mother's pregnancy. She reads him *How Babies Are Made* and Fudge then tells everyone he sees, including his nursery school class, the facts of life as he knows them. The nursery school teacher is so impressed that she calls Mrs. Hatcher and invites her to come to school and talk to the children. Larry Blume recalls that *How Babies Are Made* is the book that his mother read to him when he was about Fudge's age.

Books have always been a part of Judy Blume's life. She recalls her first experiences as a child with books. Her mother took her to the Elizabeth, New Jersey, public library and when she came home she played "library." Sheila in *Otherwise Known as Sheila the Great* tells us, "I went in to the living room. My mother was reading a book." In *Fudge-a-mania*, Fudge goes to the library looking for a book called *Tell Me a Fudge*. As a mother, Blume recalls listening to her son, Larry, "laugh when he'd get into bed at night with the Great Brain books."[12]

In *Fourth Grade Nothing* Mrs. Hatcher pulls a book off the shelf to read to the children when Fudge's birthday party begins to get out of hand. "I know . . . let's all sit down on the floor and hear a nice story," she says.

Blume has spoken of herself as a frustrated librarian. If she had become a librarian, she would have been a good one —or at least a funny one.

9

Pigeons on the Windowsill

By the time *Deenie* was published in 1973, Blume was an established author of books for children and young adults. Comparing *Deenie* to Blume's other work, Zena Sutherland, editor of the *Bulletin of the Center for Children's Books* of the University of Chicago, said, "Convincingly written in the first person this is as sensitive to a child's emotional needs and attitudes as are Blume's previous stories."[1] *Deenie* differs from Blume's other books in that she found it necessary to do research before she could begin to write. Blume visited a hospital and watched kids being fitted for body braces. The idea for the book originated when she learned of a fourteen-year-old girl who had scoliosis. Blume tells the story: "I was at a party and I was introduced to a woman who very tearfully told me about her beautiful daughter who had scoliosis and who was going to have to wear a body brace. This woman was falling apart. I asked if I could meet her daughter, and when I did, I found she was a very upbeat kid." The girl shared some of her feelings about her condition with Blume, and *Deenie* began to take shape.

Deenie is the almost-thirteen-year-old Wilmadeene Fenner, who was named after a beautiful girl her mother saw in a movie right before her daughter was born. Deenie's life is fraught with the usual teenage problems of boys, school, and family. She wants to be a cheerleader; her mother wants her to be a model. When Deenie tries out for cheerleading, a sharp-eyed gym teacher notices that something is amiss. Her parents take her to a physician, who refers her to a specialist. She is diagnosed as having, as the doctor says, "a classic case of adolescent idiopathic scoliosis." Deenie's mother is heartbroken. Her dreams for Deenie's modeling career are shattered. Deenie just wants to be like everyone else; she wants to be normal. When her father tells her she can't go to Janet's party without her brace, she runs to her room, kicks the door shut, and thinks, "I didn't want to miss Janet's party. I didn't want to miss a lot of things that would be happening in the next four years. But just tonight I wanted to be like everyone else." Slowly and painfully Deenie comes to terms with the inevitability of the body brace and its constant presence. In this process, she also learns to accept herself.

Blume was rewarded for her laborious research with a proper amount of praise. The only criticism of the book asked whether the author had perhaps provided a plethora of technical information about the disease. But Blume enjoys handing out information. In almost every one of her books one character gives another a book, a pamphlet, or information on where to go for help. It may have something to do with Blume's endless search for truth, or it may reflect her secret ambition to be a librarian. When no one explains to Deenie what scoliosis is, she takes down the *S* volume of her encyclopedia and reads about it. She writes the information in her notebook and later shares it with her friends.

Children's librarian Amy Kellman in *Teacher* comments, "In her earnestness to explain this disease which strikes young girls, the author tells the reader perhaps more about scoliosis than necessary, but she knows her characters and keeps the plot going to insure her usual large audience."[2] Similarly, well-known author Judith Viorst says, "At times this new novel runs the risk of being overwhelmed by its good intentions. I think I learned more about spines than I needed to know. But the everyday details of Deenie's world —her family, her school, her girl friends, her special boy Buddy—come through, by and large, with touching authenticity. Deenie does too."[3]

Viorst goes on to say, *"Deenie* has some fresh and honest things to say about pushy, weepy, highly imperfect mothers and about how the healthy and whole may behave toward the handicapped."[4] Deenie's mother is not one of the most likeable characters in young adult literature. In fact, many mothers react angrily to the portrayal. Blume responds by saying, "There wouldn't be the story without the mother. This is a book about parental expectations, about a mother who has categorized her children and expects them to fulfill her fantasies of what she wants to be herself."

Deenie's father demonstrates the warmth and understanding that her mother lacks. Again, Blume shows the loving relationship between father and daughter, a relationship she experienced with her own parent. It is her father that Deenie turns to when she is not selected for the cheerleading squad. He consoles her as best he can. Later in the story, after Deenie has gotten her brace, she breaks into tears when she bumps her head getting into the car. Because of the brace, she finds it difficult to bend her head. "I cried the way I wanted to when I first saw the brace, loud and hard, until my throat hurt. Daddy didn't try to stop me. He just held me tight while he rocked back and forth, patting my head."

Deenie's mother, meanwhile, avidly denies that anything can be wrong with her perfectly beautiful daughter. She says things like, "Doctors make mistakes all the time," and "No one in my family has ever had anything like this. My family's always been very healthy."

Neither of Deenie's parents is able to talk openly with her about the scoliosis. At one point, Deenie looks to her father for help, but he is busy quibbling with his wife over the injustice of the situation. Deenie says, "I wanted them to stop acting like babies and start helping me. I expected Daddy to explain everything on the way home—all that stuff Dr. Griffith had been talking about—that I didn't understand. . . . It was almost as if they'd forgotten I was there."

What makes the book more than just a story about a girl with scoliosis is Deenie's relationship with her parents.

Blume has said, "In *Deenie* my feeling was that if she had very warm, accepting, understanding parents, the story that I wanted to tell wouldn't have been there. It was not just about what was happening to her, but about the feelings and reactions of everyone around her as well."[5]

In a characteristic family scene, the four are seated at the dinner table, and Deenie is so nervous about seeing the doctor that she is unable to swallow. Deenie's mother is prodding her to eat and her older sister, Helen, jumps to Deenie's defense. Mr. Fenner then steps in on the side of his wife and the two parents talk across Deenie rather than to her. "Daddy said, 'Deenie's not worried about seeing Dr. Kliner.' 'Of course she's not,' Ma said. 'Why should she be worried? Nobody's going to do anything to her.' 'Can I be excused?' I asked."

Not only are her parents talking about her as if she were not present, they are also ignoring how she feels.

Although Deenie's sister, Helen, is in high school, she is sympathetic and caring toward her younger sibling. She brings Deenie a piece of cake and a glass of milk and asks if she wants to talk about scoliosis. Helen has been doing some research on the subject, too. In a later scene, when Deenie has her brace, Helen brings her some of her larger-sized clothes to wear—still with price tags on them. Deenie never does pour her heart out to her sister, but at least she knows she can. However, in a touching scene in one of the final chapters of the book, the two sisters cry on each other's shoulders over Helen's boyfriend. "We both cried so hard our noses ran but neither one of us let go of the other to get a tissue."

Fathers in Blume books are generally not assertive, and Mr. Fenner is no exception. Helen sums it up when she says, "Ma really burns me up sometimes! . . . I wish Daddy would tell her off just once!" In Blume's notes to herself about Deenie, she wrote, "Daddy is someone she can count on but he never stands up to Ma." This is not unlike the father in *Iggie's House*, who eventually does speak up against the petition asking the Garbers to leave the neighborhood, or the father of whom Peter Hatcher in *Tales* says, "I think my mother was relieved that my father had taken over." Mr. Fenner does assert himself when Deenie says she is not ready to go back to school after she has gotten her brace. Her mother is willing to let her stay home another day, but her father insists that she go back. " 'Deenie's going to school, same as always.' He didn't even look up from the paper. 'But Frank,' Ma said, 'if she isn't ready . . .' Daddy didn't let her finish. 'She isn't going to get any more ready sitting around the house feeling sorry for herself.' "

The relationship between Deenie and her father is strengthened even further in the final chapter of the book when Deenie tries to go to Janet's party without her brace. Her father is adamant that she wear it. "Daddy slammed the book he was reading and shouted at Ma. 'We've been through this before, Thelma.' Then he turned to me and I thought he was going to yell but when he spoke his voice was back to normal. 'The day I found out about your brace I promised myself I'd be firm,' he said. 'That's why I made you go to school when you wanted to stay home. And now I'm telling you . . . no matter how much it hurts . . . you wear the brace or you don't go.' "

Mr. Fenner has faced the tragedy that has befallen his daughter and is dealing with it. Deenie's mother continues to the end to deny that anything is wrong. She thinks somehow that if she pretends it does not exist, the problem will vanish. She does not accept the reality that Deenie has to wear the brace. Deenie's father does.

Earlier in the book, Deenie confronts her friends about their silence on the subject of her brace. "But your mother told us not to talk about it," Janet says. Deenie is irritated by her mother's attitude. "Does she think it's going to disappear if nobody says anything?"

This confrontation, which strengthens the relationship among the three girls, would not have happened if Deenie had not forced them to be honest with her. But Deenie herself has not been honest. She does not tell her friends that she is getting the brace. All they know is that she is not going to have an operation. Richard Jackson talks about the development of the relationship with Janet and Midge. "From the beginning, Deenie was a jaunty, outgoing kid, and she was right in the center of the book, but as a character she had nowhere to go. . . . Suddenly, it struck us . . . that Janet and Midge were the answer. Deenie *did* have somewhere to go in her relationship with these kids, from whom she decides to keep the truth about her illness."[6]

Jackson sees the nightgown that Janet and Midge buy Deenie as a symbol. He says, "The nightgown, an ordinary enough article, like Tony Miglione's school pennant, symbolizes a situation and expresses with simplicity a range of feelings in the story."[7] When Deenie thinks she is going to have an operation to correct her spine, her friends take her downtown and buy her lunch, treat her to a movie, and buy her a nightgown to wear in the hospital. When she finds out she will have a brace instead of the operation, she tells her friends only that she will not be having the operation. They tell her that she can keep the nightgown, but she insists on taking it back. Her friends go with her to return it, and she senses that they know something is wrong.

Another even stronger symbol of Deenie's progress toward self-acceptance is the pair of pigeons that she sees on the window ledge when she goes to talk to Mrs. Anderson, the principal. Again, Richard Jackson explains, "Those pigeons, which Deenie first sees when, in consternation, she looks away from Mrs. Anderson, which then seem to be dumbly confirming Deenie's oddity as someone handicapped, and which later have flown off, express deftly the progression of Deenie's fears and feelings about herself."

Mrs. Anderson calls Deenie to her office to talk to her about the possibility of using the bus for the handicapped. Deenie subsequently takes the note that Mrs. Anderson gives her about the bus and tears it up into very small pieces. Deenie has now accepted wearing the brace. However, she does not think of herself as handicapped, and she does not want others to think of her as handicapped either. Deenie may or may not speak *for* the handicapped, but she does speak *to* the able-bodied.

Barbara Baskin in *Notes from a Different Drummer* sums it up this way: "In a memorable scene, Deenie subtly tells readers that handicapped individuals are people just like themselves: 'This afternoon on my way to French, I didn't look away when I passed the special class. I saw Gena Courtney working at the blackboard. I wonder if she thinks of herself as a handicapped person or just a regular girl, like me.' "[8]

No discussion of *Deenie* would be complete without some mention of the *M* word: masturbation. Blume told Dr. Ruth Westheimer, renowned expert on sex and sexuality, that "of all the subjects I have written about, masturbation is the most taboo . . . especially female masturbation."[9]

Deenie worries that her scoliosis is a result of the fact that she masturbates. When another student says that she has heard that "boys who touch themselves too much can go blind or get very bad pimples or their bodies can even grow deformed," Deenie thinks, "Maybe that's why my spine started growing crooked! Please God . . . don't let it be true, I prayed." Fortunately, the levelheaded gym teacher sits down with Deenie's class and answers their questions. She explains that masturbation will not make them insane or deformed or even give them acne.

Considering, however, the myths regarding sex and sexuality that have been handed down from generation to generation, it is understandable that Deenie and her classmates worry that physical deformity results from masturbation. Patty Campbell gives us a look at late nineteenth-century thought on the subject in her book *Sex Guides: Books and Films About Sexuality for Young Adults.* She cites an 1897 volume entitled *What a Young Boy Ought to Know,* which contains the following admonition: "Self-abuse causes suffering for the boy's parents and sister, his children may be born in poverty, his offspring will be inferior because he has 'injured his reproductive powers.' The practice leads to 'idiocy, and even death.' His mind fails, his health declines, and early death ensues."[10] Masturbation as a part of a young girl's sexuality was not even discussed in 1897.

Blume says that she never heard the word *masturbation* when she was growing up and therefore is not being coy when Deenie refers to her "special place." "If I could have read *Deenie* at 12, I could have known that other kids masturbate and God I would have been relieved. I was making deals up there. It was, 'Hey, listen, I'll only do it twice this week if you'll make sure this happens and that happens.' "[11] She bristles when she hears *Deenie* referred to as "Judy Blume's book about masturbation." She says, "I didn't set out to refer to masturbation: it just grew out of the girl's character. I felt I knew her well enough to know that this is what she was doing."[12]

Deenie is not "Judy Blume's book about masturbation." It is a book about a three-dimensional character who happens, like most teenagers, to masturbate, who goes to movies and parties with her friends, and who happens to have scoliosis. Deenie's usual teenage self-centeredness is made more so by her affliction. However, Deenie matures when she begins to look outside herself and see that there are others who are truly handicapped and to realize that she can still be normal. Deenie's relationship with her father is a factor in her emotional development, and Mr. Fenner changes, too, as he comes to accept his daughter's handicap. Deenie's mother, though, continues wringing her hands and wondering where she went wrong.

10

On Trial in the Classroom

"When Randy was ten, she was a quiet, observant child," says Blume, "and terrible, terrible things were going on in her classroom. Clearly she was disturbed by it. It was not happening to her, but I think when you're an observer and you're sensitive, you know it could happen to you, and it's very frightening." Blume took her daughter's experience and turned it into a book. The book is *Blubber* (1974), and it is one of Blume's most daring pieces of writing, as daring in many ways as *Deenie,* which preceded it, and *Forever,* which followed in 1975. In *Letters to Judy,* Blume elaborates on what was going on in the classroom: "[Randy] was especially upset by the way one girl in her class, Cindy, had become the victim of the class leader. One day during lunch period, the leader of the class and her group locked Cindy in a supply closet and held a mock trial. Cindy was found guilty. 'Guilty of what?' I asked Randy at the dinner table. . . . Guilty of lack of power is my guess."[1] Blume has very strong feelings about this book. "To me, *Blubber* is one of my most important books . . . I don't think it shows how cruel kids really are. I think it just begins to touch it."[2]

Blubber is structured around three main characters: Wendy, a cruel leader; Linda, a natural victim; and Jill, the observer. Jill and her brother, Kenny, are based on Blume's own children. Jill is an avid stamp collector, as was Randy at that age, and Larry, like Kenny, could recite almost every fact from the *Guinness Book of World Records.*

The story begins with the entire fifth-grade class giving reports on mammals. Linda Fischer, who is overweight, gives her report on whales. This is a dreadful mistake. Not surprisingly, a group of classmates adopts "Blubber" as Linda's nickname. The ringleader is Wendy, who, according to Jill, is "a very clever person. Besides being class president, she is also group science leader, recess captain and head of the goldfish committee." Wendy uses her cleverness to make Linda's life miserable.

Jill becomes an unwitting participant in the cruelty early in the book when Wendy tosses her Linda's jacket as Wendy is getting off the bus. By the next chapter, however, Jill has made a calculated decision to take an active part in Linda's harassment. She does so by deciding to dress as a flenser for Halloween. A flenser, according to Linda's report, is someone who removes the blubber from whales and cuts it into strips. Wendy initiates and Jill eagerly participates in the cruelties perpetrated on Linda throughout the story. Linda is forced to undress down to her underwear in the girls' bathroom; another time she is made to eat what she is told is a chocolate-covered ant.

In the climactic scene in which Linda is put on trial by her classmates, Jill argues that Linda is entitled to a defense attorney. Wendy is appalled at this suggestion and amazed that anyone would cross her. Jill, whose father is a lawyer, is adamant that Linda deserves to be defended, saying, "If we're going to do this we're going to do it right, otherwise it's not a real trial. And since the trial was my idea in the first place I say she gets a lawyer!" Wendy vows to make Jill pay for her actions, and true to her word, she later leads the taunts directed at Jill. Linda, thankful that someone else is now the goat, gladly joins the chorus. Jill tries to laugh off the teasing, as her mother had suggested Linda might do, but it is not easy. She feels humiliated when she is the last one chosen for a team and when no one asks to be her partner for the school trip. By having been made the scapegoat Jill comes to realize how quickly roles can change and that anyone who does not go along with the group should prepare to be the next victim. Jill, however, is not willing to play martyr. Instead, she takes charge of her destiny by confronting Wendy a second time and exposing her hypocrisy in front of her friends.

Despite her positive attitude about life, Blume is a realist and a realistic writer. In *Blubber* she powerfully portrays the fact that children can be cruel to each other. In an interview with Audrey Eaglen for *Top of the News,* Blume remarked, "I think none of us realize *how* vicious [children can be]. I don't think the kind of thing Linda is subjected to is unusual; in fact, things in the real world of the fifth grade make her experience pale in comparison."[3] Blume experienced it when her son and daughter were younger. "There are children who use power in absolutely evil ways, who get drunk with power. I saw it when my kids were little, first or second grade, and the playground monitor was a fifth grader." Judy says that she was never a victim herself nor was she a mean classroom leader. She admits, however, "We were kind of mean to a kid who was said to have wet the floor, but not as awful as kids can be."

How does one child become a victim and another similar child go free? In *Blubber* we learn that Linda is "the pudgiest girl in our class, but not in our grade. Ruthellen Stark and Elizabeth Ryan are about ten times fatter than Linda, but even they can't compare to Bruce. If we had a school fat contest he would definitely win." None of these three are victims. Ruthellen, in fact, joins in the teasing of Linda on the school bus. Therefore, Linda's size is not the real issue.

Jill says, "We made Linda say, *I am Blubber, the smelly whale of class 206. . . .* It was easy to get her to do it. I think she would have done anything we said. There are some people who just make you want to see how far you can go." Richard Jackson observes: "I think Judy is saying something quite nervy in this book: that is, that there are some people who, because of the way they behave, inspire cruelty. I think one of Judy's points is that you can cast yourself into a loser role. And that's your choice. There are hangdogs and there are perkies. Linda is sort of a drip."

Blume, when pressed on this issue, replies, "I would never

say that Linda was asking for it." Blume has gotten letters from kids who have been victims year after year and are unable to do anything about it. She has also received letters from parents who have sold their homes and moved in order to remove a child from a victimizing situation. She says, "I don't think that's the answer, but I don't have the answer either." Blume does think, however, that a teacher who is aware of what is going on in his or her classroom can be instrumental in preventing the victimizing from starting in the first place. She says, "Every class has a leader but not every leader uses power in an evil way. A lot depends on the teacher. A teacher can't prevent every act of cruelty within the classroom, but he or she can go a long way in reducing it by being sensitive to the students, providing an atmosphere that is warm, secure and free from fear, and bringing the subject of how we treat each other out in the open."[4]

The picture Blume paints of the teacher, Mrs. Minish, in *Blubber* is not attractive. We see her in the early pages of the book, sitting with her head down and eyes closed, as Linda delivers her report on whales. At this point, Wendy passes around the note that reads, "Blubber is a good name for her." Minish, of course, does not see this because she is dozing.

One fifth-grade teacher wrote to Blume telling her that every fall he reads *Blubber* to his new class. He follows it with a lively discussion of the problem presented in the book and says that since he has been doing this, he has noticed a decline in the level of cruelty in the classroom and an increase in the level of caring.

Blume had some bad experiences with teachers when her children were going through the school system, but she also comes from a family of teachers. An uncle and an aunt, both of whom she admires deeply, are teachers, and she herself was trained as a teacher. She has a great respect for the art of teaching, but not the way Mrs. Minish practices it. For example, Minish marks Jill down on her math paper even though Jill has gotten the right answers, saying, "You're supposed to be learning how to think problems through and you aren't thinking the right way." Jill replies, "Isn't there more than one way to think?" Mrs. Minish reprimands her for "talking back."

When the principal comes to talk to the class about the chocolate-covered ant incident, Mrs. Minish is aghast. "I can't believe my class would act that way." Minish is once again closing her eyes, this time figuratively. Mrs. Minish allows evil to flourish by her passivity, but Miss Rothbelle, the singing teacher, is quite the active evildoer. She pulls one child's ear, raps another on the head with her ballpoint pen, and tears out "a few strands" of Linda Fischer's hair, all for no apparent reason.

If a teacher is not on the child's side, who is? What about parents? Jill says, toward the end of the story when she becomes the victim, that, "Talking to Mom on Friday night helped me feel a little better about going back to school on Monday." Jill, in fact, talks to her mother throughout the book about what is happening in school. Her mother never preaches or says, "Jill, what you and the other children are doing is wrong." She gently prods her, saying, when Jill tells her about Linda, "You should try putting yourself in her place."

There is no indication, on the other hand, that Linda has ever spoken to her mother about the situation at school. We are introduced to Linda's mother once, and that is when Mrs. Brenner meets Mrs. Fischer at a bar mitzvah. Blume says, "Children are ashamed when they're victimized. They don't come home and talk about it." Parents cannot always protect their children, but they can listen.

Linda obviously feels bad about herself. Her parents are not blamed for this, but, for whatever reason, she lacks self-esteem. At the end of the story, she still feels the same. She has apparently not changed, as she eagerly runs to Wendy's side when Jill becomes the new victim. The change, then, is in Jill, as it should be in a well-constructed novel. Jill, as the main character, is flawed. Her flaw is that she goes along with the crowd. As award-winning children's author, Marion Dane Bauer, succinctly says, "When the flawed character changes, it says to the reader, 'You can be in charge of your life.' "[5] Zena Sutherland, in the *Bulletin of the Center for Children's Books,* commented on the change in Jill, saying, "Realistically, no miracles happen. The social relationships settle down, but Linda is still an outsider and Wendy still arrogant. The change is in Jill, whose sense of values shifts to include the compassion that understanding another's position brings."[6]

Thus, Blume does not need to tell us, "Cruelty is wrong." She shows the reader by having Jill stand up to Wendy during Linda's trial. *Blubber* is typical of many of Blume's books in that she asks more questions than she answers. " 'In *Blubber,*' she says, 'I'm trying to show kids as they can be; . . . I haven't done anything about punishing the children because I would rather paint this picture of reality, to bring it out into the open and maybe then make my readers more aware.' "[7]

Children's author Marilyn Sachs caught the spirit of the book when she wrote, "This book . . . focuses on the dormant, indiscriminate cruelty of the mob and the absolute evil of any leader who uses her powers to direct that cruelty against a victim. Mrs. Blume is also saying that nobody should *allow* herself to be victimized and that Blubber's helplessness is also responsible for the gang-up."[8]

Is there, then, a moral to the story? Richard Jackson sums it up this way: "*Blubber* is, morally speaking, the toughest of all the books. That book is really about an ethical dilemma. I think it's a strong book because she doesn't say 'Cruelty is wrong!' She says, 'Cruelty hurts,' and the reader can draw his or her own conclusions."

11

Almost Grown Up

Comparisons have been made between *Wifey* (1978) and *Smart Women* (1983) and Blume's own life, and between these two books and her other writing. In many ways, the two books are different chapters from Blume's life. *Wifey* was Blume's first book for an adult audience, and although she had twelve other titles to her credit, she was insecure about writing it. "When she started writing *Wifey,* she spent lots of time second-guessing herself. Was she writing an adult story in juvenile form? Was the tone right? Were the characters convincing? The first forty pages took three months to write."[1] Why did Blume write *Wifey*? She has said that she wrote it because "it was another side of my life that I wanted to share."

If Blume was insecure writing *Wifey,* librarians were even more insecure reading about it. Children's librarians were concerned that youngsters would want to read *Wifey* simply because it was a Judy Blume book. Some children have read it and understood it. Many more have read it and not understood a word. Even more, however, have picked it up and quickly set it down, realizing this was a book they were not ready to read. Blume has been asked why she did not use a pseudonym when she wrote *Wifey*. Her reply is that she felt it would not have been honest—to herself and to her readers.

Blume wrote *Smart Women* six years after she wrote *Wifey* and after a second painful marriage and a divorce. She says that one of the reasons she wrote *Smart Women* was so that kids might read it and see that adults have problems in a divorce, too. She says, "I was trying to do the other side of the story. I have always taken the kids' side, but I know that there's another side, and it wouldn't hurt if maybe they had some understanding of what life is like for their parents." Judy's son Larry admits that he cried when he read *Smart Women*. "For the first time I stopped to think about the parents in a divorce. It never occurred to me that maybe divorced people think they've made a mistake . . . I'd only seen the kids' viewpoint."[2] Blume admits that her daughter Randy was a direct inspiration for *Smart Women*. When Randy, then a college freshman, met George Cooper, one of the first things she asked him was if he had heard about her mother's man-of-the-month club. George, not missing a beat, answered that he had but that the others were alternate selections.[3]

Wifey was a purgative of sorts for Blume and as such is full of biographical details of her life as Mrs. John M. Blume. Blume's brother says that her writing has saved her thousands of dollars and thousands of hours on the psychiatrist's couch. *Wifey* disposes of the dregs of a former life, the suburban housewife, and *Smart Women* analyzes a new lifestyle.

Here is the old Judy Blume: in *Wifey*, we learn early in the story that Sandy Pressman has been sick, that she has tried golf and tennis lessons, and that she throws plates to soothe her anger. Blume was ill much of the time before she began writing. She took golf and tennis lessons and failed at them, and she "went through a lot of crockery."

Blume has said, "If you want to know about my illnesses, read *Wifey*." Indeed, they are all here. The childhood diseases: "She had lain in bed for two weeks that time, listening to soap operas on her radio, doing movie star cut out books, reading Nancy Drew mysteries." Her high school illness: eczema. Her college illness: mono. "Everybody else had plain old acne but Sandy suffered through eczema like patches all over her body. . . . And then, as a college freshman, mono." Marriage was for Sandy, and for Judy, "a never-ending parade of physical problems."

While Sandy is busy being ill, Norman, her husband, is concerned only about his golf game. Sandy's mother is brought in to help with the children, "because in eleven and a half years of marriage he had never missed a day of work or a golf or tennis game." Blume says that when her first book was accepted for publication, "I did the unspeakable. I called him [John] at the golf course."

If Sandy so despised the game of golf, why did she continue taking lessons? She asks herself the same question and answers, "Because she was expected to. Because she always did what she was told. Because she was such a good little girl. Such a good little wifey." Blume says, "I grew up being a good little girl, always trying to please."

Although they are pleasing the world on the outside, Sandy and Judy have ways of getting even. When it comes to politics, Sandy says, "He thought his politics were her politics; his candidate, her candidate. Oh, the thrill of pulling the lever for Kennedy, defying Norman, even secretly!" Blume's son Larry likes to tell the story of the first time his mother voted in a presidential election. She had dutifully placed telephone calls for the Republican presidential candidate and then quietly voted for the Democrat.

Despite Blume's trepidation in writing *Wifey*, the final result was a book that received surprisingly favorable reviews. *Publishers Weekly* announced, "With this novel, Judy Blume proves she can write as effectively for adults as she does for children" and called the book "perceptive and funny."[4]

Joyce Smothers in *Library Journal* said, "Blume's dialogue sparkles, and she skillfully evokes a comfortable middle-class atmosphere."[5] *Best Sellers'* Eve Simson, apparently missing the joke of the entire story, wrote, "The author manages, perhaps unintentionally, to convey a view of suburban life as a dehumanizing existence."[6]

Although it provoked some naysayers, *Smart Women*, Blume's second novel for adults, was received with more adulation than the first. Blume, in attempting to objectively

portray the adults' point of view, created the most vital teenage characters of her career. She herself says of Michelle,
Margo's daughter, "I never knew I'd love her so much."

There are essentially four main characters in *Smart
Women* around whom other characters radiate: Margo,
B.B., Margo's daughter, Michelle, and B.B.'s daughter Sara.
Sara is starting junior high and Michelle is sixteen. B.B.
owns her own real estate agency and Margo is an architect;
both are successful at what they do. Margo has one other
child, a son, Stuart, who is a year older than Michelle.

B.B. had a son who was killed in a car accident when he
was ten. His death haunts B.B. "Bobby was dead. Dead on
Arrival. Ten years old and still wearing his little league uni-
form and his new cleats." She blames her ex-husband, Andrew, for the boy's death. He had been driving the station
wagon full of kids home from their game when the accident
occurred. Her anger grows when Andrew moves in next
door to Margo, and the real trouble begins when he moves
in *with* her.

A lack of honesty is apparent in B.B.'s denial of Bobby's
death. "How come Mom had to pretend that Bobby was
never born?" Sara asked. "So that she could pretend that he
never died," Daddy answered. In trying to keep the truth of
the accident inside, B.B. finds that it eats away at her, first
destroying her relationship with her husband and eventually
shattering her own life.

When B.B. meets Lewis, a man who loves her, she does
not tell him about Bobby. "She wondered if she could spend
the rest of her life pretending. Pretending to be happy. Pretending to be the most together person he had ever known.
It was so hard to pretend. It took up almost all of her en-
ergy. Sometimes she felt so tired from pretending that she
just wanted to let go, to slip away quietly, to let the warm
ocean water cover her and carry her away."

Later, when B.B. is hospitalized following her nervous
breakdown, she tells a friend who is visiting her that she had
a son who died in an automobile accident. She concludes,

"I'm learning to deal with the truth. That's why I'm here. And from now on would you call me Francine? That's my real name."

While B.B., or Francine, is learning to deal with the truth, people around her continue to avoid it. Sara, her daughter, is not told that her mother married Lewis, and Margo and Andrew disagree on whether or not she should be told. Margo argues that "she should be told the truth about everything," saying, "I don't like secrets, Andrew. Secrets always backfire." Sara, assessing the problem squarely, thinks, "Oh, she hated grownups and all their secrets!" Again and again, Blume points out that adults can and should be straightforward with children.

Blume feels that the teenage girls in this book are two of the best characters she has ever written. Reviewers agree. "As in all Miss Blume's books, the voices of the children ring loudest and clearest. While her adult characters often seem contrived and one-dimensional (not to mention depressing), the children are splendid in their richness," says Linda Bird Francke in the *New York Times*.[7] She continues, "Margo's 16-year-old daughter, Michelle, is worth the whole book when her mother announces that B.B.'s ex-husband Andrew is moving in with them. Michelle 'couldn't breathe.' "[8] Patricia Bosworth in *Working Women* says, "All the teenagers are beautifully portrayed— . . . Sara, in particular, as the angry, emotionally blocked preteen, is astonishingly real. . . . At last a novel that doesn't discuss money, power and sex, but friendship, families, caring and pain."[9]

Little, if any, blatant sex occurs in *Smart Women*, but some men who read the book have found Margo threatening because of her habit of keeping a list of her lovers. Blume says, "They no doubt disliked her because she acted so much like the stereotypical *man*, separated, freely indulging in sex-without-strings, seemingly detached."[10]

The sex scenes in *Wifey* are not subtle. There are detailed descriptions of Sandy's sexual encounters. Blume defends these scenes in the same way she defends *Are You There God?* or *Deenie*. "I see my book as being very realistic, and as ludicrous as many of Sandy's thoughts are, people have ludicrous thoughts, and I think we should write about it more—so that people who have these thoughts can read it and say, 'ah-h-h-h, I'm not the only one. I'm so glad.' "[11]

No Blume book is complete without a plug for sex education. In *Smart Women* it occurs when Puffin, Stuart's girlfriend, becomes pregnant. She comes to talk to Michelle about it. Michelle explains to Puffin that there is no safe time. Puffin says, "I know that now." Michelle helps arrange for the abortion and generally acts as the adult through the entire ordeal. Later, Puffin's mother and Margo chat casually at lunch one day about the sex education pamphlets they have each given their children. Both are, sadly, unaware of what has taken place.

Michelle exhibits the most change in the course of the story. As the novel begins, she is generally sullen and angry with her mother about almost everything. By the end of the book Michelle has gained some insight into her mother's problems and has begun to think of someone besides herself. The culmination of Michelle's maturation occurs when she is helpful and understanding toward Sara when Sara has her first period. After coaching her through the physical part, Michelle goes a step further and to help Sara feel good about herself, bakes her a chocolate cake with the inscription, "Congratulations, Sara." Michelle has come a long way, considering that in the beginning of the story, she commonly referred to Sara as "the Brat." Michelle is not unlike other Blume characters such as Deenie or Jill, who, through their own turmoil develop compassion and understanding of those around them.

Margo cares about B.B. early in the story, although she admits it is difficult to get close to her. B.B., on finding out that Andrew is moving to town, takes to her bed. Margo decides to make her chicken soup to cheer her up. She phones her mother in New York, who is on her way to Lincoln Center for the ballet, to get the recipe.

Margo's mother is the tap dancing grandmother who began taking lessons at the age of sixty-two. "She took three lessons a week, inspired by Ruby Keeler's performance in a revival of *No, No, Nanette*. And she was good." This is, of course, none other than the Judy Blume of the future. At the anniversary party, "Grandma put on the gold tap shoes that Grandpa had given to her for their golden wedding anniversary and she did a number to 'You Are My Lucky Star,' with double pullbacks and everything."

The Judy Blume of *Wifey* is not the same person as Margo in *Smart Women*. *Wifey* was written by a woman who was bitter about her marriage and about her divorce. It is in many ways an angry book. Judy Blume grew up some in the time between that book and *Smart Women*. She says, "When I wrote *Wifey*, . . . I had stopped believing in the possibility of monogamous, long-term relationships. . . . My life with George has led me to believe that it *is* possible." *Smart Women* is a culmination of Blume's growth as a woman and as a writer that began with *Are You There God? It's Me, Margaret*. Lynne Hamilton charges that "Behind *Wifey*'s weak and unhappy central figure, Sandy Pressman . . . it is not hard to see a Margaret, a Deenie, a Davey or a Katherine."[12] There is, in truth, no evidence to support such a statement. Margaret, Deenie, Davey, and Katherine would never aspire to be "wifeys," although they may grow up to be "smart women." And even smart women fall in love.

12

Una Buena Aventura

"Each of us must confront our own fears, must come face to face with them. How we handle our fears will determine where we go with the rest of our lives. To experience adventure or to be limited by the fear of it." This is the theme of the Judy Blume novel that is her son Larry's favorite book and that began its life as a screenplay. The book is *Tiger Eyes* (1981).

Blume tells the story of how *Tiger Eyes* came to be written:

I was in Santa Fe. My second marriage had ended disastrously, and I wanted a change. Along came a group of producers who wanted me to write a screenplay for a TV movie of the week. I was thrilled. I had never done a screenplay before. They came to Santa Fe and wooed me. I told them the story I had in mind and they said "Great." But when I wrote the screenplay and they had read it, they said, "We ordered a Judy Blume story, and we didn't get one." I wanted to cry or throw up. I was so upset. I was terribly hurt. They wanted to change everything about the story and I couldn't do that. I am a realistic writer and things have to be right. It is a story about violence and the aftermath of violence, and they wanted the father to die of a heart attack spelunking in northern New Mexico. There are no caves in northern New Mexico. I told the producers that I could not do another draft, and instead I wrote the book. The book was quite successful, and the producers came back and said, "Let's make a movie of the book." So we started again. But by then I was working on another book and they brought someone else in to collaborate with me, but when it was finished it went into a drawer at NBC and sat for five years. Luckily they never did anything with it, and the rights came back to me. Larry will make *Tiger Eyes* into a movie some day.

A rather harrowing beginning for a book that is something of a sleeper. In some ways the producers were right. *Tiger Eyes* is not a typical Judy Blume story. It is certainly the most political of any of her books; it is also the most serious and the most thoughtful. Blume uses the book to wrap up several of the loose ends of her life: her fears, the death of her father, and her search for adventure.

Early in the story, Davey Wexler is immobilized by fear. She is unable to get out of bed, except to go to the bathroom; she has not eaten or bathed in thirteen days. Davey is not the only one in her family who is afraid.

Her younger brother, Jason, climbs in bed with their mother and asks if the guys who shot Daddy will come back and shoot them, too. Mrs. Wexler reassures Jason that they are perfectly safe, but Davey knows that she keeps a loaded gun under her bed, and Davey has a bread knife under her pillow. She lies awake listening for footsteps on the outside stairs (they live above the 7-Eleven store where her father was killed some days before). They leave a light on in every room. Fear is the underlying current, the overriding theme of *Tiger Eyes*—the fear of violence, of strangers, of danger, and the greatest of all, of annihilation. Childhood fears, says Blume, may actually be heightened by adults' attempts to hide them. She says, "I hate the idea that you should always protect children. They live in the same world we do. They see things and hear things. The worst is when there are secrets, because what they imagine, and have to deal with alone, is usually scarier than the truth. Sexuality and death —those are the two big secrets we try to keep from children, partly because the adult world isn't comfortable with them either. But it certainly hasn't kept kids from being frightened of those things."[1]

As the book opens, Davey is rummaging through her closet for a pair of shoes to wear to a funeral. Coming up with nothing suitable, she borrows a pair of three-inch spike heels from her mother. At the grave site, along with learning the realistic details of the heat forming a pool of sweat in Davey's bra and the blisters growing on her feet, we learn that it is Davey's father's body that is being lowered into the ground.

When Davey's friend, Lenaya, comes bearing condolences, we find out from the stack of newspaper clippings piled on Davey's bed that Davey's father, Adam Wexler, was gunned down by an unknown assailant who robbed his 7-Eleven store. We also come to know that Aunt Bitsy (who is Mr. Wexler's sister) and her husband, Uncle Walter, have arrived from Los Alamos to be with the family during this difficult time and that Aunt Bitsy is busy making sandwiches, which Davey cannot eat.

A young man who worked at the store comes to visit Davey, and she grudgingly goes for a walk on the beach with him. When he tries to kiss her, she breaks from him and runs home. She goes to bed and stays there for five days.

On the eve of the new school term, Davey's mother convinces her to shower and wash her hair. Davey's younger brother, Jason, is eagerly looking forward to beginning second grade, and Mom lets him wear his Dracula cape because it makes him feel "comfortable." With the help of Lenaya, Davey manages to get to school, but once there she makes it through two classes before collapsing in the hallway. When it is obvious that Davey cannot survive a day at school without fainting, the family doctor recommends a change of scenery.

Jason, Davey, and Mom head for the "safe" and loving arms of Aunt Bitsy and Uncle Walter in Los Alamos. Jason attaches himself immediately to Aunt Bitsy, and the two of them find solace in cookie dough. Mom, with the aid of her headache medicine, crawls into bed and stays there, while Davey is ready to be alone with her feelings. While exploring a desert canyon, Davey meets Wolf, a quiet, thoughtful young man who is a student at Cal Tech.

Just before the family is to return to Atlantic City, they are notified that the store has been vandalized. Mrs. Wexler becomes hysterical, and Walter and Bitsy convince her to stay a while longer. Mom retreats deeper into her medication.

Bitsy enrolls Davey in school, where she meets Jane, who is smart and wealthy but fearful and alcoholic. Jane is a candystriper at a local hospital, and Davey decides she would like to be one, too. At the hospital she encounters Mr. Ortiz, who is dying of cancer and who, it turns out, is Wolf's father. The two of them indirectly help Davey to work through her anger, grief, and fear. After several sessions with a counselor, Mom too is at last ready to return to Atlantic City and get on with her life.

Blume was perhaps ready to get on with her own life when she wrote *Tiger Eyes.* She had suffered through two years of a horrendous marriage, had divorced her second husband, and in order to provide some stability for her children, was staying in New Mexico. Larry was in high school when she was writing *Tiger Eyes,* and she recalls: "I was trying to finish the book, and at one point, there were so many kids in the house that I had to rent a motel room in order to work."

Work she did, but not all agree that the results were worthwhile. Gay Andrews Dillin in the *Christian Science Monitor* faults the book for its realism with these words: "*Tiger Eyes* may not be as popular with readers as some other Blume books. It deals with an ugly subject and could create unnecessary fears in some young people."[2] Blume says that "unnecessary fears" are caused by sweeping "ugly subjects" under the rug. In her words, "I think the more you bring things to the surface, even unpleasant things, the easier they become to deal with."[3]

An example of how adults refuse to acknowledge ugliness occurs in this revealing dinner table scene. Mom joins the family for dinner for the first time in a week. " 'I'm not myself,' Mom says. 'I'm not the person I used to be before Adam . . .' Her voice trails off and there is a heavy silence at the table. It is the first time she has said his name out loud in front of us. 'Before Adam . . .' she tries again, but her voice breaks. 'Died,' I say. Everyone looks at me. I feel my cheeks flush. Then everyone looks away as if I have broken some deep, dark secret. Jason goes back to tapping his fork against the table." Aunt Bitsy tries to erase the discomfort by serving them each a good-sized portion of chicken tetrazzini.

The year proceeds and it is Christmas time, the first Christmas without Adam. But they don't talk about it, Davey notices. Because of this veil of silence, Mom is unable to talk to anyone in the family about her feelings, and keeping all this grief inside is giving her terrible headaches. Bitsy finally convinces her to see a counselor, and Davey, in an attempt to force her mother to face reality, confronts her about her sessions with Miriam, the therapist. When Mom admits that she talks about the murder in therapy, Davey wonders why she can talk about it to Miriam but not to her.

Although Davey is fifteen when her father dies and Judy was twenty-one, it is nevertheless a natural outcome of Blume's life that she wrote one of her most significant books about death. "Her father's sudden death from a heart attack at the age of 54 made Judy realize what a fragile thing life really was. . . . When he died, part of Judy died, too. . . . Now she said goodbye, too, to that warm, safe feeling she had had so many years ago when she snuggled in her father's arms."[4]

The setting of *Tiger Eyes* is taken from Blume's own experience, too. She lived in Los Alamos for two years during her second marriage, and later moved to Santa Fe. Setting *Tiger Eyes* in New Mexico was a major shift for Blume. She says, "I think we write best about the things we really do know about. I set most of my books in suburban New Jersey because this is where I grew up. And I think that when it is very real to you, it is very real to your readers."[5] But in order for Blume's irony about death to come through, it was necessary for the bulk of this story to be set in Los Alamos, the site of the development of the atomic bomb. As Margaret Mason in the *Washington Post Book World* points out, "Davey, her mother, and seven-year-old brother are struggling to come to grips with decimating, anonymous violence while seeking security in Los Alamos (the Atomic City)."[6] By placing the story here Blume is carrying out the theme of fear and sharing with the reader the ultimate fear, the fear of the bomb. To further the irony, Blume dots the setting with a number of churches. Mason suggests that "Davey, with the acute eye of the young, is disdainfully aware of the hypocrisy of, among other things, a middle class which designs bombs during the week and worships on Sundays. There are more churches in Los Alamos than I have ever seen anywhere."[7]

Uncle Walter, as the bomb builder, is the personification of evil, yet he is surely not the devil as we, or Davey, had pictured him. Davey says, when she first meets Walter, that she always thought a weapon designer would be hard and cruel. "A kind of wild-eyed mad scientist, intent on blowing up the world. But Walter is so ordinary. I just can't get over the fact that he is somehow involved in building bombs. In killing people." Even the name "Walter" is benign, a fit name for a man who plays the viola in a chamber music group. That, Blume is saying, is what makes the Walters of the world all the more terrifying. As Davey questions him on his part in the weapons design, Walter explains, "Think of us as watchdogs, Davey, making sure that no one will ever attack us. But if they really do, we'll be ready. And being ready is more than half the battle." Davey counters, "But if nobody made bombs in the first place . . ." Walter assures her that that would be lovely, but it is plainly not the way the world is.

In a finely tuned juxtaposition of comedy and tragedy, Davey later tries to think of Walter as a watchdog, but the only picture she gets in her mind is of a German shepherd, or a Doberman, named Walter. As she did in Atlantic City, Davey tucks the bread knife under her pillow and sleeps with one hand wrapped around it. Davey is still afraid, but this fear is on a much grander scale.

The irony is further played out in Walter's (and Bitsy's) own fears, which, of course, have nothing to do with the bomb. They are full of stories about what might happen and don't believe in taking chances. "They will probably live to be 100," says Davey. As Pamela Pollack in *School Library Journal* described them: "Walter and Bitsy leave nothing to chance; they're believers in bicycle helmets, bomb shelters, and bran flakes."[8]

Bitsy is well meaning but not very smart. She's the "yes, dear" type of spouse who doesn't want any trouble and is willing to go along with whatever Walter decides. Bitsy is proud of her husband's work—she's a tour guide at the bomb plant. If Walter had worked at Auschwitz, Bitsy would have conducted tours of the ovens. If Walter's life is a sin of commission, Bitsy's is one of omission. When Davey is leaving Los Alamos, she says to Bitsy, *"La vida es una buena aventura."* Bitsy understands neither the language nor on any other level what Davey is talking about. She responds, after Davey translates for her ("Life is a great adventure"), "Sometimes it is and sometimes it isn't." It seems that for Bitsy, most of the time it isn't.

The couple's fears are further exemplified by their resistance to allowing Davey to learn to ski or to drive. Finally, Davey's anger comes to a head, and she explodes at Walter: "You're a good one to talk. . . . You're the one who's making the bombs. You're the one who's figuring out how to blow up the whole world. But you won't let me take driver's ed. A person can get killed crossing the street. A person can get killed minding his own store." In this one scene, Davey brings it all together: her anger with her father for dying, her anger with her mother for not interceding with Walter, and her anger at Walter for building bombs to destroy the earth.

Davey's anger with her mother has been building for some time. One night when Davey goes to her mother's room to complain about Walter, she finds her asleep, with photos of Adam scattered across the bed. She feels so angry she wants to shake her. Earlier in the book, when Bitsy takes Davey to enroll in school, she thinks to herself that the wave of anger she feels is not really for Bitsy but for her own mother "home in bed, zonked out on headache medicine."

Davey's anger at her father surfaces the first time she meets Wolf. Wolf challenges her on it, saying, "Who are you so pissed off at anyway?" "The world!," Davey tells him, without even thinking about it. She is surprised by her answer to his question. It is the first time she has realized she is not only sad about her father but angry at his death and angry at his murderer. Blume offers an insight into this emotion: "That anger when you say, 'Don't be dead, Daddy. Please let it be a big mistake. I need you and I want you.' And you never really get over that.'"

Davey resolves her anger with her mother first by venting her displeasure toward her. When Davey demands that she stop taking the headache medicine, daughter and mother have, in effect, traded places. Davey is beginning to take charge, not only of her own life but also of her mother's. This insight into the faults of grownups is part of the maturing process. Davey remembers that when she was unable to get out of bed, her mother was there to help her. Looking beyond her own problems and thinking about how to help another person is also the beginning of Davey's growth and change.

Little by little, Mom is able to get herself together and to confront her own fears. It is not a coincidence that the first meal Mrs. Wexler fixes since her husband's death is spinach pie, the same meal she prepared the night of his death. This is her way of reliving the night, within a warm and loving environment, in order to put it to rest. Mom finally reaches the point where she is ready to leave Los Alamos and return to Atlantic City. Davey tells her, "I'm glad you're not afraid anymore, Mom." Mom answers, "Who says I'm not afraid?" As Mrs. Wexler prepares to leave Los Alamos, Bitsy puts in one last word of warning, protesting that Atlantic City is not safe. Mom bravely asserts that she can't let safety and security become the focus of her life. Bitsy chooses the safety and security of Los Alamos.

In one especially picturesque and telling scene, Blume gives us a critical insight into the personalities of her four main characters. The setting is the annual hot air balloon festival at Albuquerque, which in this novel is a symbol for life and active participation in it. Bitsy says the event is beautiful to watch but only a fool would participate. Walter insists that it is a moot point because it will never happen. It certainly is never going to happen for Walter and Bitsy, who are watchers. Davey says she would go up in a balloon in a minute. Davey is a risk taker and a survivor, and we have a clue here that no matter what happens, she will choose life. Jason, wanting to do anything that Davey would do, says that he would go too, and Mom, with perhaps the saddest commentary of all, says that she would like to go up and never come down.

Another level of fearfulness is apparent in Davey's friend, Jane. The girls are shopping in Santa Fe when they pass a group of Spanish-speaking boys. Davey wonders aloud, for Jane's benefit, how much of the two-way racial hatred she has experienced in New Mexico is caused by fear. By telling Jane how foolish it is to be afraid of people you do not know, Davey demonstrates that she has overcome many of her own fears and is now willing to help Jane overcome hers. Jane is afraid of boys, so she drinks to keep up her courage on a date. Toward the end of the story, Davey tells Jane to be honest with herself and to confront her alcoholism. Jane retorts that Davey was not honest when she told Jane that her father died of a heart attack. As Davey is getting ready to leave Los Alamos and return to Atlantic City, Jane says that she will probably spend the rest of her life in Los Alamos because she is afraid not to. Davey reminds her once more that she must stop being scared. Working past her own depression to help another human being aids Davey in her own recovery.

Davey's relationship with her brother Jason is not to be taken lightly. Jason's role in the story is not merely comic relief. Davey's concern and love for him are signs of her growing maturity. She is beginning to care about someone other than herself and something other than her own pain. When Mrs. Wexler is in the midst of her depression and Jason worries that she too will die, Davey is able to comfort him in the night. "He comes closer to my bed and I reach out and hug him. 'It's going to be all right,' I whisper into his hair. 'It is . . . it is . . . it is . . .'" One cannot help but make the comparison with Holden Caulfield in *Catcher in the Rye,* who in his daydream watches children playing in a cliff-top rye field and catches them when they stray too near the edge. Davey, in protecting Jason from straying too near the edge, is at the same time saving her own life.

Wolf plays a major part in Davey's recovery. He gives her the impetus to go on with her life, but she must ultimately be the one to choose. In one of the most powerful scenes in the book, Davey sits on the edge of the canyon and contemplates her own death, marveling at how quickly life can come to an end. With Walter and Bitsy's countless warnings ringing in her ears, she climbs down into the canyon and calls to her dead father. The voice that answers is that of Wolf.

Critic Lynne Hamilton faults Blume for too hastily filling the gap in Davey's life. "Her handling of death and loss seems dishonest. Davey never fully experiences what it means to be without a father. Wolf, the boyfriend, who plays the key role in Davey's recovery, is in many ways a father surrogate."[10] To some extent, this is true. After her encounter with Wolf, Davey races home and gobbles up the chicken sandwich that Bitsy left for her. She is hungry for the first time since her father's death. She then gets into the shower and sings—again, something she has not done since the tragedy.

It is important, however, to look beyond Wolf's immediate effect on Davey to the death of Wolf's father and the far-reaching effect that has on her. Note, too, that as Davey scrambles down the rocks, she wishes she could share the experience with her father, to tell him how she climbed down into the canyon by herself and was not afraid. Thus, even before Wolf enters the scene, Davey has accomplished something on her own and, more important, has begun to overcome some of her own fears.

The death of Mr. Ortiz is the culmination and final act in Davey's recovery. Blume packs it with symbolism that is tight and effective. When Davey first meets Mr. Ortiz, he tells her that he is dying of cancer and that he is ready to die because he has been in and out of the hospital too many times, for too long. Davey turns and looks out the window —the sun is setting—and wonders bitterly why he had to tell her he is dying. The sunset might be a cliché in any other setting, but in this scene it is potent.

Another simple but stunning symbol is a dancing wind-up bear that Wolf has given his father. On the day that Davey finds out that Wolf and Mr. Ortiz's son are the same person, "Wolf winds up the bear and sets it on the table, where it dances in circles, until it wears down, moving more and more slowly until it stops completely. Like Mr. Ortiz, I think."

Not unlike the dancing bear in symbolism is the candle that Davey buys as a Christmas gift in memory of her father. He had a habit, she says, of collecting unusual candles and lighting them for special occasions. The candle depicts the New Mexican sunset, in all its glorious color. On Christmas night before going to bed Davey takes out the candle and lights all five wicks on it and watches as the New Mexican sunset disappears. "Merry Christmas, Daddy," she thinks. "I wish you were here." In fifteen minutes, nothing is left except a pile of wax. Margaret Mason aptly calls this "one of the most poignant and healing scenes in the book."[11]

When Mr. Ortiz dies, Davey is able to release the torrent of emotions that have built up inside her. When she comes to his room one afternoon and he is gone, she rushes down the hall to the nurse's station, only to find out that he died during the night. A nurse hands her the dancing bear and an envelope with a note from Wolf. She puts the note back in its envelope and holds the toy to her face. "I can't stop crying. I am crying harder now than when my father died. Then, I was just numb. Now I feel everything."

Later, with Miriam, the counselor, Davey is able to relive the night her father died. In a final act of mourning, she rushes home, takes the brown paper bag from the closet, the bag containing the blood-soaked clothes, and rides to the canyon and buries the clothes, along with the bread knife, under a pile of rocks. She says goodbye to her father, promising to remember him full of life and full of love. This was how Wolf asks her to remember *his* father.

Davey has confronted her fears. She has come face to face with them. Davey has chosen life and will continue to choose adventure. *La vida es una buena aventura.*

13

Mirror, Mirror, on the Wall

On one side of a debate that continues to rage among critics of young adult literature is British author and critic David Rees bemoaning the lack of quality in Blume's writing in his article "Not Even for a One-Night Stand": "Perhaps the best thing to do with Ms. Blume would be to ignore her altogether; she is so amazingly trivial and second-rate in every department—the quality of her English, her ability to portray character, to unfold narrative—but that is impossible: she is 'controversial' on both sides of the Atlantic; and her work is read and discussed not only by the young but by those adults who have a serious concern for children's literature."[1] On the other side of the debate is Faith McNulty, writing glowingly in the *New Yorker* that "As in a play, dialogue carries the story along. It is colloquial, often funny, and always revealing. Blume doesn't waste words. Her stories are told in the first person sustained soliloquies that are prodigies of total recall."[2]

Blume's writing has been criticized from every angle. Although few critics have come forward to support Blume's writing, because Blume dares to write about sensitive subjects, she has been attacked by many conservative authorities in the field of children's literature.

To understand this widespread critical assault, it is necessary to examine Blume's place in the field of young adult literature. To begin with, Blume is a writer of realistic fiction. *Time* magazine writer J. D. Reed aptly dubbed her the "godmother of upscale adolescent realism."[3] Then there is the difficulty of distinguishing the realistic novel from the problem novel. Blume's characters clearly do have problems. Her books do not become problem novels because the stories do not focus on the problem but on the protagonists' resolution of the problem. Characters are the essential ingredient in a Blume novel. As Richard Jackson notes, "Each of her main characters faces a problem, but none of her books is about the problem; each is about a kid or kids in a real situation, facing it in his or her own way."[4] Norma Klein observed in an article entitled "More Realism for Children": "Whenever you say you are interested in realistic fiction which deals with modern themes, people assume you mean something grim, what has come to be known as 'problem' books. That very term is revealing; it shows the extent to which we still regard any aspect of sexual development as negative, perforce a 'problem.' "[5] Even renowned children's author Beverly Cleary has explained that she does not write problem novels: "I'm more interested in writing about people than problems. *Dear Mr. Henshaw* is about a boy that had a problem, not a problem that had a boy. I don't search for a new problem."[6]

This emphasis on the distinction between a realistic novel and a problem novel may seem trivial, but confusion between the two has led to serious misunderstanding of Blume's work. Sheila Egoff's definition in an article entitled "The Problem Novel" may prove helpful. "Problem novels have to do with externals, with how things look rather than how things are. They differ from the realistic novel in their limited aim, which is to tell rather than show."[7] Blume, as a realistic novelist, does the reverse. "Show, don't tell," she says, "That's the one thing I think about every day. I learned *that* from Dick." Jackson says, "Judy doesn't tell, because her characters don't tell. They don't say, 'Now watch, dear reader, what Tony's mother does to him next.' It's not necessary, because we see what Tony's mother does next. Judy shows and doesn't tell because she's dealing with first-person kids who are not guiding us through a novel. The characters would be quite surprised if you stopped them and said, 'Do you know you're in a novel?' Those stories happen because the characters have something very important going on for them."

Realistic fiction for young adults came into its own in the late sixties with S. E. Hinton's *The Outsiders* and Paul Zindel's *The Pigman* leading the charge. Robert Cormier appeared in the seventies, along with M. E. Kerr, Richard Peck, and Norma Klein. In the midst of them all was Judy Blume. Blume, the writer, had found her niche. It was her place and her time.

But something about this new realism of the late sixties and early seventies bothered some teachers and librarians. These books seemed to be too adolescent centered. The young people in the Zindel novels seemed to have no parents at all, Peck's characters seemed not to have homes, and all of them spoke to the reader in the first person. The author of the *New York Times Book Review* article "A New Cycle in 'YA' Books" observed that "starting in the late 60's, a new kind of book for teens began to appear, reflecting a changing balance of power between the generations. The domestic upheavals of the late 60's shook the traditional faith that adults could provide sure moral guidance or a safe haven for the young."[8]

Faith McNulty, a convert to Blume-ism, wrote in praise of the author's brand of veracity: "In a Judy Blume book, realism is everything. True, it has no great depth, but it is extraordinarily convincing. True, she includes unpleasant details—things we all notice but usually don't mention—yet they increase the credibility that is the source of her magnetic power. Blume's technique might be compared to *cinema verité*. She writes as though filming the landscape of childhood from the eye level of a child. She focuses on nearby objects and immediate events with a child's intense gaze, picking out details that evoke instant recognition." McNulty goes on to talk about Blume's use of the first-person narrative style, which is a key technique of the realistic style in adolescent literature. "Each book begins on a note of candor. We have the feeling of reading a secret diary

—something the writer intended only for himself. Thus, it seems natural when usually private matters are included. Often, they are things that have to do with the dawning of sex, and though most are quite innocuous it is a shock to see them suddenly exposed in print. The effect is a mesmerizing intimacy, which convinces Blume's readers that she writes the whole truth about what kids think and feel."[9]

Blume does speak straight to her audience. She says that in many ways she is acting when she is writing and that much of the story comes about by pretending. Jackson describes it as "speaking directly into the ear of the reader." The first-person narrator technique is the backbone of Blume's writing, and its effectiveness is evidenced by her many imitators. Though she was not the first to use this method, she was one of the first to use it well. Jackson says the reason that the first-person voice is effective in Blume's books is "that the characters all have something on their minds. First person is not a gimmick," he goes on, "it is an impulse."

Agnes Perkins of Eastern Michigan University complains that "The first person teen-age narrator is a technique frequently used by American writers and may be one reason many of the books are not first-rate; it is a very difficult voice to sustain without hitting a false note or boring a reader to weariness." She claims Mark Twain and J. D. Salinger are the only two American authors who have been able to carry out the style adequately.[10] For Blume the first-person style is her own, and she has perfected it. Blume the writer never intrudes on her character's thoughts. We get to know Tony and Margaret, Deenie and Davey, and all the others as they are and as they know themselves.

Blume is not a narrative writer. We come to know the characters and their surroundings through their dialogue. Jackson says, "The British reviewers go crazy because there's no description. Judy doesn't like description. I asked her in *Tiger Eyes* to describe the ocean. She wrote it and she hated it and we cut it. It is not something she does with any comfort, nor does she believe it's necessary." Again, Blume shows through dialogue rather than tells. Her readers seem to find that seeing and hearing what happens is certainly more interesting than being told what is happening.

"The triviality of her thinking is matched by the sheer shoddiness of her English," says David Rees of Blume's style. "She employs the usual sub-Salingerese American first-person narration, but so unmemorably that it makes Paul Zindel's use of the technique look like startling originality. There is absolutely nothing in Judy Blume's style that defines it as specifically hers."[11] R. A. Siegal, in an article entitled "Are You There God? It's Me, Me, Me" in *The Lion and the Unicorn,* praised Blume's style on the one hand—"Blume's most characteristic technique and the key to her success is the first-person narrative. . . . All her books read like diaries or journals and the reader is drawn in by the narrator's self-revelations"[12]—and damned it on the other—"Since all her books are told through the voice of a child narrator, the vocabulary is necessarily limited and the sentence construction basic and repetitious."[13]

Blume says, "My ideas come from real life, and then I go with them. . . . What I really am is a character and a dialogue writer. That's where I'm strongest. All my books are just a matter of time and place and situation and how characters deal with each other. They're about how we all change."[14] Lynn Hamilton writes in *Signal,* a British journal of literary criticism, that quite the opposite is true. She analyzes four of Blume's most popular novels, *Are You There God? It's Me, Margaret., Deenie, Tiger Eyes,* and *Forever.* She argues that "Blume demystifies the purported 'crises.' Pain, religion, death, and sex, she says in effect, are 'no big deal.' Her young heroines are given the answers before they have had a chance to grapple with the questions. By reducing, dismissing, or denying the crises, Blume prevents them from occasioning passage. Her heroines adjust and cope; they do not suffer and change."[15]

Blume's characters, however, do fill out, not only physically but emotionally as well, until they are quite well rounded. Deenie and Davey, in particular, grow and change in the course of their stories. Her father's love is a positive force in Deenie's life, and Wolf, the young college student, helps Davey see that life is worth living. Essentially, however, both Davey and Deenie find an innate strength within themselves. Blume's characters may not suffer the poverty and cruelty inflicted on the characters in a Dickens novel, yet they do suffer the helplessness of youth. Critics who claim that Blume's protagonists do not experience pain are like Tony's mother who says, "What problems? A thirteen-year-old boy doesn't have any problems!"

Blume's heroes and heroines depict the powerlessness of childhood. Decisions are made without their input—decisions about jobs, new babies, and relocation of the family. However, they are not abandoned by their loved ones, as Saku Repo in *Canadian Dimensions* would make them out to be. "The children of Judy Blume are alone in a much more profound sense than orphan Anne Shirley ever was at the lowest point in her life. They can count on nothing but their own resources in figuring out how to survive with some integrity."[16] This is simply not true. Even in the worst family situations—*It's Not the End of the World,* for example—Karen has a best friend that she can count on, and she has a younger sibling who needs her, and those two people are essential to Karen's survival. "The parent-child relationships," says Richard Jackson, "are always very interesting. All of her books contain very sustaining family situations—even the ones that are falling apart."

There is a vigorous sense of caring and kindliness in Blume's fiction that is not present in the work of other writers. Big sisters comfort younger siblings in *Just As Long As We're Together, Tiger Eyes,* and *It's Not the End of the World.* Katherine, in *Forever,* tells her parents that she is keeping an eye on her younger sister at camp. Katherine's parents, too, are loving and understanding. Jill's mother, in *Blubber,* listens and gives astute advice. Blume has been criticized for not dealing with moral issues. What could be more virtuous than a warm, caring family relationship? Blume has said, "I expect to write about those subjects that are important to me. And what is especially important are human relationships."[17]

The youthful characters in Blume's stories are concerned about people other than themselves. Katherine, in *Forever*, volunteers in the geriatric unit of the hospital; Davey, in *Tiger Eyes*, is a candy-striper. Tony, in *Then Again, Maybe I Won't*, is sensitive to other people's problems to the point that it makes him ill. Margaret, in *Are You There God? It's Me, Margaret*, is aware of her Jewish father's feelings when her Protestant grandparents come to visit. These youngsters reinforce the argument that Blume's characters are not, as Philomena Hauck has said, "self-absorbed and preoccupied with their own feelings and affairs,"[18] or as Professor Mary Burns said, "always concerned with themselves—a narcissistic attitude in vogue among many of the young in the United States today."[19] R. A. Siegal, who may have introduced the word *narcissism* in the critical literature on Blume, became quite emphatic in his condemnation: "What seems important to note here, however, is that self-consciousness is offered as a model for children to identify with and that self-awareness and the awareness of other people's feelings are presented as goals in themselves. . . . Self-consciousness and self-awareness, however, can turn rapidly into self-absorption. Blume's books are remarkable in the number of narcissistic incidents they portray: Margaret examining herself in a mirror, Tony's masturbation, and so on."[20] Naomi Decter took up the cry in *Commentary*, saying, "Miss Blume is as much a creature of her times and class spiritually as she is sexually. The consistent and overriding message of her books . . . is that the proper focus of one's curiosity and concern is oneself."[21] Librarians, not to be outdone, sent Jack Forman to the front: "Young adults should be encouraged to look past their navels at the same time that they are given strong support to their changing lives."[22]

Narcissism is a normal part of the maturation process. Teens and preteens may spend an inordinate amount of time thinking about themselves and their relationship to the world. Adults often forget having gone through this stage of development. Young people also may exhibit an intense interest in their bodies as major hormonal changes occur. To ignore these physical and intellectual changes would be to deny life itself. Author Judith Viorst shed some light on the topic of narcissism in her book *Necessary Losses*. Freud's thinking on narcissism, she says, was that "the more we loved ourself, the less we could love another. He said love of self and other were opposed. And he left us with the impression that narcissism most certainly wasn't a good thing." She continued, "In recent years, however, some psychoanalysts—particularly Heinz Kohut—have challenged this negative, polarized view of narcissism. Narcissism, says Kohut, is normal, is healthy, is important, is a good thing. And a hearty love of self will enrich and complement—not deplete—our love of others."[23]

Recently journalist Michele Landsberg put forth the thesis that at the root of Blume's and S. E. Hinton's narcissistic writing styles are their assertions that neither could find books about kids like themselves when they were growing up. She concludes, "Their almost identical statements lay bare an almost identical narcissism, as well as an astonishingly limited knowledge of available children's literature."[24] Landsberg continued, "What may indeed corrupt the children . . . is not Blume's frankness, but her bland and unquestioning acceptance of majority values, of conformity, consumerism, materialism, unbounded narcissism, and flat, sloppy, ungrammatical, inexpressive speech."[25] Landsberg's criticism would be more convincing if it were accurate. She states, for example, that "Mothers never go out to work in Blume books except in dire emergency, and then they are resented by their children. Fathers are usually more caring than mothers, though equally characterless. No one in Blume ever reads a novel, thinks about any sphere of human congress beyond the classroom or bedroom, or rises above a materialistic self-absorption."[26] Landsberg evidently overlooked Katherine's mother in *Forever,* who is a children's librarian, and the scene in *Blubber* where Jill's mother gets a run in her pantyhose as she is hurriedly getting dressed for work. She also failed to cite the scene in *Blubber* in which Jill says, "That night, after my bath, I went to my parents' room. Mom was stretched out reading a book," and the scene in *Otherwise Known as Sheila the Great* where Sheila says, "I went into the living room then. My mother was reading a book."

The debate over literary value may continue for as long as Blume's works are in print. Teachers and librarians and parents have to decide whether to take advantage of the popularity of the books or to attempt to undermine their impact. Even Blume's harshest critics may conclude that these books can at least be used to lead youngsters to more traditional material. Philomena Hauck has proposed this compromise: "Instead of ignoring the books or being ultracritical of them, teachers and librarians will have to adopt a different stance. They should become thoroughly familiar with the Blume books. . . . Then they can talk to young people about them and gradually lead their young charges to become more critical and perceptive. . . . They can take them from where they are to other similar books which will bring greater insight and satisfaction."[27] Don Gallo has advised teachers that "We do our students as well as ourselves a disservice if . . . we dismiss Judy Blume as a shallow writer because she writes as kids talk, uses one-dimensional characters, and deals with topics previously considered taboo by proper people."[28] Many other critics, including Faith McNulty, are grateful to Blume for having "convinced millions of young people that truth can be found in a book and that reading is fun."[29]

In more than twenty years the Blume titles have garnered

more criticism than books by any other author of books for children and young adults. Teachers and librarians and critics may debate the pros and cons of Blume books, but youngsters continue to read them. As Ursula Nordstrom has so wisely said, "The children are new, though we are not." Richard Jackson quotes Blume as saying, "There will always be fear and hope, love and hate, jealousy and joy . . . because feelings belong to everyone. They are the link between the child of today and the children we were."[30]

Appendix:
Awards Won by Blume's Books

Are You There God? It's Me, Margaret.

1980 – Great Stone Face Book Award, New Hampshire Library Association
1979 – North Dakota Children's Choice Book Award
1976 – Young Hoosier Book Award, Indiana
1975 – Nene Award from the Children of Hawaii
1974 – Wisconsin Golden Archer Award

Blubber

1983 – North Dakota Children's Choice Book Award
1977 – Young Readers' Choice Award of the Pacific Northwest

Freckle Juice

1980 – Michigan Young Readers' Award, Michigan Council of Teachers

Just As Long As We're Together

1989 – Young Readers' List, Virginia State Reading Association

Otherwise Known as Sheila the Great

1984 – Book of the Month Award, German Academy for Children's and Young People's Literature
1982 – South Carolina Children's Book Award
1978 – South Carolina Children's Book Award

The Pain and the Great One

1986 – Young Readers' Choice Award, Alabama Library Association

1985 – Children's Choices, International Reading Association and Children's Book Council Committee

Superfudge

1989 – Favorite Book of the Children of Michigan, Michigan Reading Association

1988 – Favorite Book of the Children of Missouri Award, Missouri State Library; The Soaring Eagle Award, Wyoming Educational Media Association

1986 – Great Stone Face Book Award, New Hampshire Library Association; Young Readers' Choice Award, Alabama Library Association

1985 – Great Stone Face Book Award, New Hampshire Library Association; Sunshine State Young Reader's Award, Florida Association for Media in Education

1984 – Reader's Choice Award, Washington County, Minnesota; New Mexico Land of Enchantment Children's Book Award, New Mexico International Reading and Library Associations

1983 – Northern Territory Young Readers' Book Award, Darwin, Australia; Garden State Children's Book Award, New Jersey Library Association; Iowa Children's Choice Award; Arizona Young Readers' Award; Georgia Children's Book Award; California Young Reader Medal; Young Readers' Choice Award, Pacific Northwest Library Association, Edmonton, Alberta, Canada; Young Hoosier Book Award, Merrillville, Indiana; Golden Sower Award, Nebraska Library Association; Great Stone Face Book Award, New Hampshire Library Association

1982 – Utah Children's Book Award; Texas Bluebonnet Award; Sue Hefley Book Award, Louisiana Association of School Libraries; Tennessee Children's Choice Book Award; Colorado Children's Book Award; North Dakota Children's Choice Book Award; Nene Award from the Children of Hawaii; West Australian Young Readers' Book Award; Georgia Children's Book Award; First Buckeye Children's Book Award, Columbus, Ohio; US Army in Europe Kinderbuch Award

1981 – Great Stone Face Award, New Hampshire Library Council; Children's Choice Award, International Reading Association and Children's Book Council; Michigan Young Readers' Award, Michigan Council of Teachers

1980 – Texas Bluebonnet Award

Tales of a Fourth Grade Nothing

1983 – Massachusetts Children's Book Award

1981 – Great Stone Face Award, New Hampshire Library Council; USAREUR Kinderbuch Award, U.S. Army & 7th Army, Heidelberg, Germany

1980 – West Australian Young Readers' Book Award; North Dakota Children's Choice Book Award

1978 – Rhode Island Library Association Award

1977 – South Carolina Children's Book Award; Georgia Children's Book Award; Massachusetts Children's Book Award; Arizona Young Readers' Award, Arizona State University

1975 – Pacific Northwest Library Association Young Readers' Choice

1972 – Charlie May Swann Children's Book Award

Tiger Eyes

1985 – Iowa Teen Award, Iowa Educational Media Association; Colorado Blue Spruce Young Adult Book Award

1983 – Dorothy Canfield Fisher Children's Book Award, Montpelier, Vermont; Buckeye Children's Book Award; Columbus, Ohio; California Young Reader Medal

1982 – Books for the Teen Age, New York Public Library

1981 – A Best Book for Young Adults, School Library Journal

Other Awards

1990 – Favorite Author, Children's Choice Award, Harris County, Texas

1989 – "Most Admired Author," Heroes of Young America Poll, World Almanac
– Children's Choice Award, New Jersey Region III
– Favorite Author, Children's Choice Award, Harris County, Texas

1988 – South Australian Youth (S.A.Y.) Media Award for Best Author, from South Australian Association for Media Education

1988 – Favorite Author, Children's Choice Award, Harris County, Texas

1987 – Honorary Doctorate of Humane Letters, Kean College, Union, New Jersey; Favorite Author, Children's Choice Award, Harris County, Texas; "Award for Excellence" in the field of literature, New Jersey Educational Association

1986 – Civil Liberties Award, American Civil Liberties Union of Atlanta, Georgia; John Rock Award, Center for Population Options, Los Angeles; State of New Jersey honoree, for significant contribution to the history of New Jersey's women

1985 – Favorite Author, Children's Choice Award, North Olympic Library System, Washington; Favorite Author, Children's Choice Award, Harris County, Texas; Appreciation Award, Girls Clubs of America

1984 – Carl Sandburg Freedom to Read Award, Chicago Public Library; Favorite Author, Children's Choice Award, Harris County, Texas

1983 – Jeremiah Ludington Memorial Award, Educational Paperback Association; Milner Award, Atlanta Public Library; Favorite Author, Children's Choice Award, Harris County, Texas; Eleanor Roosevelt Humanitarian Award

1981 – Today's Woman Award (for achievement in the liter-

ary field), Council of Cerebral Palsy Auxiliaries of
Nassau County, New York
1974 – Golden Archer Award

Film Awards
Otherwise Known as Sheila the Great
1989 – Crystal Apple (top award), National Educational
Film and Video
– Finalist, American Film & Video Festival
– Finalist, Film and TV Festival, New York
– Finalist, USA Short Film Festival
– Finalist, Chicago International Festival of Children's
Films

Notes and References

Chapter 1

1. "1975 Sequoyah Award Acceptance Speech," *Oklahoma Librarian* (October 1975):7.

2. Kathleen Hinton-Braaten, "Writing for Kids Without Kidding Around," *Christian Science Monitor,* 14 May 1979, B10.

Chapter 2

1. J. D. Reed, "Packaging the Facts of Life," *Time,* 23 August 1982, 65.

2. Faith McNulty, "Children's Books for Christmas," *New Yorker,* 5 December 1983, 193.

3. Claire M. Smith, letter to author, 2 May 1988.

4. Barbara Ann Porte, "Point of View: What Is It about Books by Judy Blume?," *Advocate* (Fall 1982):44.

5. Hinton-Braaten, "Writing for Kids," B10.

6. Diane Roback, "Children's Books: A Junior High," *Publishers Weekly,* 19 June 1987, 83.

7. Children's Book Council, *Children's Books: Awards and Prizes* (New York: Children's Book Council, 1986), 129.

8. Ibid., 121.

9. Ibid., 38.

10. *Reading Teacher* (November 1975):129.

11. Barbara Elleman, "Chosen by Children," *Booklist,* 1 December 1982, 507.

12. Ibid.

13. Don Gallo, "What Should Teachers Know about YA Lit for 2004?," *English Journal* (November 1984):32.

14. Ibid.

15. Claire M. Smith, letter to author, 2 May 1988.

16. Gallo, "What Should Teachers Know," 32.

17. Kenneth L. Donelson and Alleen Pace Nilsen, *Literature for Today's Young Adults* (Glenview, Ill.: Scott, Foresman, 1985), 102.

18. Philomena Hauck, "Judy Blume and Beyond," paper presented at the annual meeting of the Canadian Council of Teachers of English, Saskatoon, Canada, August 1982, 9.

19. Robert Mayer, "The Blume Generation," *Rocky Mountain Magazine* (January–February 1982):72.

20. Jane Power, "Meet Judy Blume; Kid's-eye View Draws Students . . . and Censors," *NEA Today* (October 1984):11.

21. Allen Raymond, "Judy Blume Tells It Like It Is . . . and That's Why Kids Love Her," *Early Years* (May 1984):24.

22. "Judy Blume: Gold Medalist with Kids Tells How to Finish First," *Instructor* (November 1979):62.

23. Judith Higgins and Amy Kellman, "I Like Judy Blume. It's Like She Knows Me," *Teacher* (January 1979):72.

24. Porte, "Point of View," 44.

25. Stephen Garber, "Judy Blume: New Classicism for Kids," *English Journal* (April 1984):56.

26. Judith M. Goldberger, "Judy Blume: Target of the Censor," *Newsletter on Intellectual Freedom* (May 1981):61.

Chapter 3

1. "Report Finds Censorship Still on Rise," *Newsletter on Intellectual Freedom* (November 1987):219.

2. Ken Donelson, "Almost 13 Years of Book Protests . . . Now What?," *School Library Journal* (March 1985):97.

3. Mark Canter, "Book Bannings Have Increased 107 Percent in 5 Years," *Bradenton [Florida] Herald,* 31 May 1987.

4. Allene Symons, "Censorship—a Clear and Present Danger," *Publishers Weekly,* 21 June 1985, 60.

5. People for the American Way, *Attacks on the Freedom to Learn,* 1986–1987 Report, 3.

6. Lincoln S. Bates, "Empty Shelves in Georgia," *Progressive* (December 1986):17.

7. "Censorship Still on Rise," 219.

8. Paula C. Saunders, "Judy Blume as Herself," *Writer's Digest* (February 1979):21.

9. *Newsletter on Intellectual Freedom* (March 1985):42.

10. *Newsletter on Intellectual Freedom* (January 1985):8.

11. Ibid., 9.

12. *Newsletter on Intellectual Freedom* (January 1983):21.

13. *Newsletter on Intellectual Freedom* (March 1985):59.

14. "ACLU Appeals *Deenie* Ban," *School Library Journal* (December 1985):11.

15. Pro Family Forum "X-Rated Children's Books" (Fort Worth, Texas).

16. Ibid.

17. Dorothy M. Broderick, "Censorship: A Family Affair?," in *Young Adult Literature: Background and Criticism,* ed. Millicent Lenz and Ramona Mahood (Chicago: American Library Association, 1980), 466.

18. Gay Andrews Dillin, "Judy Blume: Children's Author in a Grown-Up Controversy," *Christian Science Monitor,* 29 December 1981, B5.

19. Mark I. West, "What Is Fit for Children?," *New York Times Book Review,* 24 August 1986, 20.

20. Power, "Meet Judy Blume," 11.

21. Judy Blume, "What Kids Want to Read," *Principal* (January 1982):7.

22. Goldberger, "Target of the Censor," 62.

23. Robert Cormier, "Forever Pedaling on the Road to Realism," in *Celebrating Children's Books: Essays on Children's Literature in Honor of Zena Sutherland,* ed. Betsy Hearne and Marilyn Kay (New York: Lothrop, Lee & Shepard, 1981), 48.

24. Randy Sue Coburn, "The Big Deal about Blume," *Washington Post Magazine,* 16 June 1985, 20.

25. Porte, "Point of View," 46.

26. "Old Values Surface in Blume Country," *Interracial Books for Children Bulletin* 7, no. 5 (1976):9.

27. Audrey Eaglen, "Answers from Blume Country: An Interview with Judy Blume," *Top of the News* (Spring 1978):240.

28. Ibid.

29. "Old Values," 10.

30. Goldberger, "Target of the Censor," 81.

31. *Newsletter on Intellectual Freedom* (January 1987):31.

32. *Newsletter on Intellectual Freedom* (May 1980):51.

33. *Newsletter on Intellectual Freedom* (July 1983):121.

34. *Newsletter on Intellectual Freedom* (November 1984):185.

35. *Newsletter on Intellectual Freedom* (September 1985):167.

36. *Newsletter on Intellectual Freedom* (January 1983):21.

37. *Newsletter on Intellectual Freedom* (November 1982):205.

38. *Newsletter on Intellectual Freedom* (May 1982):83.

39. *Newsletter on Intellectual Freedom* (January 1985):8.

40. "Authors Protest Peoria Ban on Blume Books," *Publishers Weekly,* 7 December 1984, 21.

41. *Newsletter on Intellectual Freedom* (November 1985):193.

42. *"Deenie* Ban," *School Library Journal,* 11.

43. Bates, "Empty Shelves," 17.

44. *Newsletter on Intellectual Freedom* (September 1983):139.

45. *Newsletter on Intellectual Freedom* (May 1983):71.

46. "Free Access to Libraries for Minors: An Interpretation of the Library Bill of Rights," in *Intellectual Freedom for Children: A Packet of Materials,* compiled by the Association for Library Service to Children, a division of the American Library Association, April 1984, 31.

47. "Q&A on Censorship," American Library Association, n.d. 4.

48. "Free Access to Information for Young Adults," American Library Association, 22 January 1978.

49. *Newsletter on Intellectual Freedom* (November 1985):193.

50. *Newsletter on Intellectual Freedom* (March 1986):57.

51. "Peoria School Board Restores Blume Books," *Publishers Weekly,* 21 December 1984, 26.

52. *Newsletter on Intellectual Freedom* (September 1983):153.

53. *Newsletter on Intellectual Freedom* (January 1981):20.

54. *Newsletter on Intellectual Freedom* (March 1983):37.

55. *Newsletter on Intellectual Freedom* (January 1987):31.

56. *Newsletter on Intellectual Freedom* (September 1985):167.

57. McNulty, "Children's Books," 191.

58. *Newsletter on Intellectual Freedom* (January 1981):20.

59. *Newsletter on Intellectual Freedom* (January 1985):9.

60. "What Kids Want," 7.

61. Joe Adcock, "SCT Will Be in Full Blume Tonight," *Seattle Post-Intelligencer,* 13 March 1987.

62. "Phil Donahue Show," 2 March 1982 (videotape).

63. Power, "Meet Judy Blume," 11.

64. Goldberger, "Target of the Censor," 62.

65. "Censorship or Selection: Choosing Books for Public Schools," produced by Media and Society Seminars in association with the Intellectual Freedom Committee of the American Library Association and the Association of American Publishers, New York, Media and Society Seminars, 1983 (videotape).

Chapter 4

1. Review of *Forever, Junior Bookshelf* (February 1977):49.

2. Myra P. Sadker and David M. Sadker, *Now upon a*

Time: A Contemporary View of Children's Literature (New York: Harper & Row, 1977), 63.

3. Eaglen, "Blume Country," 242.

4. Joyce Maynard, "Coming of Age with Judy Blume," *New York Times Magazine,* 3 December 1978, 90.

5. John Gough, "Reconsidering Judy Blume's Young Adult Novel *Forever,*" *Use of English* (Spring 1985):33.

6. Patty Campbell, *Sex Guides: Books and Films about Sexuality for Young Adults* (New York: Garland Publishing, 1986), 223.

7. Alice P. Naylor and Carol Wintercorn, *American Writers for Children since 1960: Fiction,* ed. Glenn E. Estes (Detroit: Gale Research Co., 1986), 34.

8. Lou Willett Stanek, "Just Listening: Interviews with Six Adolescent Novelists," *Arizona English Bulletin* (April 1976):36.

9. Pamela Pollack, "Sex in Children's Fiction: Freedom to Frighten?," *Siecus Report* (May 1977):16.

10. McNulty, "Children's Books," 201.

11. "Children's Author—Judy Blume," 16mm, 17 min. (New York: National Broadcasting Company, 1980). Distributed by Films, Inc.

12. Maynard, "Coming of Age," 84.

13. Jane Quinn, "Communicating with Pre-Adolescents," *Siecus Report* (March 1984):9.

14. Jean Fredricks, conversation with author, Duluth, Minnesota, July 1987.

15. Mary S. Calderone, M.D., "Review of *Forever,*" *Siecus Report* (May 1977):9.

16. Donelson and Nilsen, *Literature,* 401.

17. "Children's Author," 1980.

18. Campbell, *Sex Guides,* 226.

19. Gough, "Blume's Young Adult Novel," 32.

20. Dorothy Nimmo, "Review of *Forever,*" *School Librarian* (December 1976):335.

21. Audrey Eaglen, " 'Where Did You Go?' 'To the Li-

brary.' 'What Did You Get?' 'Nothing' " *Siecus Report* (19):2.

22. David Rees, "Not Even for a One Night Stand: Judy Blume," in *The Marble in the Water: Essays on Contemporary Writers of Fiction for Children and Young Adults* (Boston: Horn Book, 1980), 180.

23. Nicholas Tucker, "Bedtime Stories," *Times Literary Supplement,* 1 October 1976, 1238.

24. Peter Kennerley, ed., *Teenage Reading* (London: Ward Lock Educational, 1979), 154.

25. Ibid., 170.

26. Frank Bataglia, "If We Can't Trust: The Pertinence of Judy Blume's *Forever,*" in *Celebrating Censored Books,* ed. Nicholas J. Karolides and Lee Burress (Racine: Wisconsin Council of Teachers of English, 1985), 43.

27. Calderone, review of *Forever,* 9.

28. Dillin, "Grown-Up Controversy," B5.

29. Donelson and Nilsen, *Literature,* 23.

30. Coburn, "Big Deal," 20.

31. Ibid.

32. John J. O'Connor, film review of *Forever, New York Times,* 6 January 1978, C21.

33. Kevin Thomas, " 'Forever': Story of a First Love," *Los Angeles Times,* 6 January 1978, IV24.

Chapter 5

1. Eaglen, "Blume Country," 237.

2. Stanek, "Just Listening," 36.

3. Diana Gleasner, *Breakthrough: Women in Writing* (New York: Walker, 1980), 20.

4. Barbara Rollock, "The World of Children's Literature," radio interview with Judy Blume, New York, WNYC, 31 November 1977.

5. Ibid.

6. Ibid.

7. John Neary, "The 'Jacqueline Susann of Kids'

Books,' Judy Blume, Grows Up with an Adult Novel," *People Weekly*, 16 October 1978, 54.

8. Jean Mercier, review of *Starring Sally J. Freedman as Herself*, *Publishers Weekly*, 18 April 1977, 62.

9. Diane Haas, review of *Starring Sally J. Freedman as Herself*, *School Library Journal* (May 1977):59.

10. Rollock, "World of Children's Literature."

11. Haas, review of *Sally*, 59.

12. Rollock, "World of Children's Literature."

13. Review of *Starring Sally J. Freedman as Herself*, *Junior Bookshelf* (August 1983):169.

14. Margaret O'Connell, "Paperbacks: One Gulliver Step," *New York Times Book Review*, 5 November 1972, 42.

15. Dorothy Broderick, review of *Are You There God? It's Me, Margaret.*, *New York Times Book Review*, 8 November 1970, 14.

16. Review of *Are You There God? It's Me, Margaret.*, *Publishers Weekly*, 11 January 1971, 62.

17. Jeanette Daane, Review of *Are You There God? It's Me, Margaret.*, *School Library Journal* (December 1970):42.

18. Ann Evans, "Blood and Tears" (review of *Are You There God? It's Me, Margaret.*), *Times Literary Supplement*, 7 April 1978, 383.

19. Stanek, "Just Listening," 37.

20. Rollock, "World of Children's Literature."

21. Sheila Egoff, *Thursday's Child: Trends and Patterns in Contemporary Children's Literature* (Chicago: American Library Association, 1981), 69.

22. Hauck, "Blume and Beyond," 8.

23. Agnes Perkins, "What Books Should Be Sent to Coventry? A Comparison of Recent British and American Realistic Fiction," paper presented at the Sixth Annual Conference of the Children's Literature Association, University of Toronto, March 1979, 161.

24. Jon Shapiro and Geraldine Snyder, "Et Tu, Judy Blume: Are the Books Girls Choose to Read Sexist?," *Reading Horizons* (Summer 1982):245.

25. Susan N. Smith, "Father Doesn't Know Best Anymore: Realism and the Parent in the Junior Works of Judy Blume, E. L. Konigsburg, and Richard Peck," paper presented to the faculty of the Graduate School of Stephen F. Austin State University, Nacogdoches, Texas, August 1981, 62.

26. Julia Whedon, review of *Starring Sally J. Freedman as Herself, New York Times Book Review,* 1 May 1977, 40.

27. Shapiro and Snyder, "Et Tu, Judy Blume," 244.

28. Ibid.

29. Ibid.

30. Ibid., 245.

31. John R. Townsend, *Written for Children* (Boston: Horn Book, 1974), 279.

32. Broderick, review of *Are You There God?,* 14.

Chapter 6

1. Lucy E. Waddey, "Cinderella and the Pigman: Why Kids Read Blume and Zindel Novels," *ALAN Review* (Winter 1983):7.

2. McNulty, "Children's Books," 201.

3. "Old Values," 10.

4. Eaglen, "Blume Country," 238.

5. Roy Blatchford, review of *Then Again, Maybe I Won't, Times Educational Supplement,* 18 January 1980, 43.

6. Power, "Meet Judy Blume," 11.

7. Smith, "Father Doesn't Know Best," 65.

8. Julia Kagan, "What They Really Want to Know," *McCall's* (June 1979):100.

9. Marsha Kay Seff, "Kid Talk or Soft Porn?," *St. Paul Dispatch,* 22 December 1980, 16A.

Chapter 7

1. *Letters to Judy: What Your Kids Wish They Could Tell You* (New York: Putnam's, 1986), 91.

2. "Meet Judy Blume," brochure, Bradbury & Dutton, n.d.

3. Bonnie McGee, "Seeing the Child's Side: An Interview with Judy Blume," *Forecast* (October–November 1981):50.

4. Richard W. Jackson, "Books That Blume: An Appreciation," *Elementary English* (September 1974):781.

5. Sadker and Sadker, *Now upon a Time,* 31.

6. *Letters to Judy,* 102.

7. Jane Resh Thomas, review of *Just As Long As We're Together, Star Tribune,* 18 October 1987, 8Gx.

8. Josephine Humphreys, Review of *Just As Long As We're Together, New York Times Book Review,* 8 November 1987, 33.

Chapter 8

1. "Sequoyah Award," 7.

2. Review of *Tales of a Fourth Grade Nothing, Booklist,* 1 July 1972, 941.

3. "Sequoyah Award," 7.

4. Power, "Meet Judy Blume," 10.

5. Cyndi Pock, Seattle Children's Theatre, interview with author, Seattle, Washington, August 1987.

6. Beverly Cleary, in *Through the Eyes of a Child: An Introduction to Children's Literature* by Donna E. Norton (Columbus: Merrill, 1987), 414.

7. "Sequoyah Award," 7.

8. Linda Johnson, "Review of *Otherwise Known as Sheila the Great,*" *School Library Journal* (May 1973):69.

9. Eaglen, "Blume Country," 237.

10. Review of *Otherwise Known as Sheila the Great, Publishers Weekly,* 14 August 1972, 46.

11. Smith, "Father Doesn't Know Best," 61.

12. McGee, "Seeing the Child's Side," 50.

Chapter 9

1. Zena Sutherland, *Bulletin of the Center for Children's Books* (April 1974):123.

2. Amy Kellman, review of *Deenie, Teacher* (January 1974):112.

3. Judith Viorst, review of *Deenie, New York Times Book Review,* 4 November 1973, 46.

4. Ibid.

5. Justin Wintle and Emma Fisher, "Judy Blume," in *The Pied Pipers* (New York: Paddington Press, 1974), 313.

6. Jackson, "Books That Blume," 782.

7. Ibid.

8. Barbara Baskin, *Notes from a Different Drummer: A Guide to Juvenile Fiction Portraying the Handicapped* (New York: Bowker, 1977), 123.

9. Dr. Ruth Westheimer, "The All New Dr. Ruth Show," 10 May 1987.

10. Campbell, *Sex Guides,* 10.

11. Anne Commire, ed., *Something about the Author* (Detroit: Gale, 1983), 31–34.

12. Wintle and Fisher, *Pied Pipers,* 315.

Chapter 10

1. *Letters to Judy,* 45.

2. Dillin, "Grown-Up Controversy," B5.

3. Eaglen, "Blume Country," 236.

4. *Letters to Judy,* 49.

5. Marion Dane Bauer, speech at Minnesota Society of Children's Book Writers' Conference, Minneapolis, 7 November 1987.

6. Zena Sutherland, review of *Blubber, Bulletin of the Center for Children's Books* (May 1975):142.

7. Eaglen, "Blume Country," 234.

8. Marilyn Sachs, review of *Blubber, New York Times Book Review,* 3 November 1974, 42.

Chapter 11

1. Gleasner, "Breakthrough," 41.

2. Carla Waldemar, "Author and Her Material Grow Up," *Twin Cities Reader,* 7 March 1984, 27.

3. Coburn, "Big Deal," 21.

4. Review of *Wifey, Publishers Weekly,* 31 July 1978, 90.

5. Joyce Smothers, review of *Wifey, Library Journal,* 1 September 1978, 1659.

6. Eve Simson, review of *Wifey, Best Sellers,* January 1979, 295.

7. Linda Bird Francke, review of *Smart Women, New York Times,* 19 February 1984, 27.

8. Ibid.

9. Patricia Bosworth, review of *Smart Women, Working Woman* (March 1984):178.

10. D. Fortino, "Beware the Casual Fling," *Harper's Bazaar* (July 1984):44.

11. Hinton-Braaten, "Writing for Kids," B10.

12. Lynne Hamilton, "Blume's Adolescents: Coming of Age in Limbo," *Signal* (May 1983):94.

Chapter 12

1. Maynard, "Coming of Age," 91.

2. Gay Andrews Dillin, review of *Tiger Eyes, Christian Science Monitor,* 14 December 1981, B10.

3. Eaglen, "Blume Country," 240.

4. Betsy Lee, *Judy Blume's Story* (Minneapolis: Dillon, 1981), 78.

5. Wintle and Fisher, *Pied Pipers,* 311.

6. Margaret Mason, "Judy Blume: Growing Up with Grief," *Washington Post,* 13 September 1981, 9.

7. Ibid.

8. Pamela D. Pollack, review of *Tiger Eyes, School Library Journal* (November 1981):100.

9. Sandy Rovner, "Judy Blume," *Minneapolis Star,* 12 January 1982, 3C.

10. Hamilton, "Blume's Adolescents," 90.

11. Mason, "Growing Up with Grief," 10.

Chapter 13

1. Rees, "One Night Stand," 173.
2. McNulty, "Children's Books," 193.
3. Reed, "Facts of Life," 65.
4. Jackson, "Books That Blume," 781.
5. Norma Klein, "More Realism for Children," *Top of the News* (April 1975):310.
6. Cleary, *Through the Eyes of a Child*, 381.
7. Sheila Egoff, "The Problem Novel," in *Only Connect: Readings on Children's Literature*, ed. Sheila Egoff, G. T. Stubbs, and L. F. Ashley. (New York: Oxford University Press, 1980), 357.
8. "A New Cycle in 'YA' Books," *New York Times Book Review*, 17 June 1984, 24.
9. McNulty, "Children's Books," 193.
10. Perkins, "What Books Should Be Sent to Coventry?," 158.
11. Rees, "One Night Stand," 175.
12. R. A. Siegal, "Are You There God? It's Me, Me, Me," *Lion and the Unicorn* (Fall 1978):74.
13. Ibid., 73.
14. Archie Bridge, "Judy Blume Jumps the Generation Gap: Young Readers' Favorite Novelist Writes a New Book for Adults," *Book & Author* (March–April 1984):24.
15. Hamilton, "Blume's Adolescents," 88.
16. Satu Repo, "From Green Gables to Suburbia," *Canadian Dimension* (April 1981):47.
17. Donelson and Nilsen, *Literature*, 394.
18. Hauck, "Blume and Beyond," 7.
19. Dillin, "Grown-Up Controversy," B5.
20. Siegel, "It's Me, Me, Me," 75.
21. Naomi Decter, "Judy Blume's Children," *Commentary* (March 1980):66.
22. Jack Forman, "Young Adult Books: Watch Out for #1," *Horn Book* (January–February 1985):85.
23. Judith Viorst, *Necessary Losses* (New York: Ballantine, 1986), 54.

24. Michele Landsberg, *Reading for the Love of It: Best Books for Young Readers* (New York: Prentice-Hall, 1987), 205.

25. Ibid., 207.

26. Ibid., 210.

27. Hauck, "Blume and Beyond," 12.

28. Gallo, "What Should Teachers Know," 32.

29. McNulty, "Children's Books," 201.

30. Jackson, "Books That Blume," 783.

Selected Bibliography

PRIMARY WORKS

Novels

Are You There God? It's Me, Margaret. Englewood Cliffs, N.J.: Bradbury, 1970; Dell, 1972.

Blubber. Scarsdale, N.Y.: Bradbury, 1974; Dell, 1977.

Deenie. Scarsdale, N.Y.: Bradbury, 1973; Dell, 1974.

Forever. Scarsdale, N.Y.: Bradbury, 1975; Pocket, 1976.

Freckle Juice. New York: Four Winds, 1971; Dell, 1978.

Fudge-a-mania. New York: Dutton, 1990; Dell, 1991.

Iggie's House. Englewood Cliffs, N.J.: Bradbury, 1970; Dell, 1976.

It's Not the End of the World. Scarsdale, N.Y.: Bradbury, 1972; Dell, 1982.

Just As Long As We're Together. New York: Orchard Books, 1987; Dell, 1988.

The One in the Middle Is the Green Kangaroo. Chicago: Reilly & Lee, 1969; Dell, 1982.

Otherwise Known as Sheila the Great. New York: Dutton, 1972; Dell, 1976.

The Pain and the Great One. Scarsdale, N.Y.: Bradbury, 1984; Dell, 1985.

Smart Women. New York: Putnam's, 1983; Pocket, 1984.

Starring Sally J. Freedman as Herself. Scarsdale, N.Y.: Bradbury, 1977; Dell, 1978.

Superfudge. New York: Dutton, 1980; Dell, 1981.

Tales of a Fourth Grade Nothing. New York: Dutton, 1972; Dell, 1976.

Then Again, Maybe I Won't. Scarsdale, N.Y.: Bradbury, 1971; Dell, 1973.

Tiger Eyes. Scarsdale, N.Y.: Bradbury, 1981; Dell, 1982.

Wifey. New York: Putnam's, 1978; Pocket, 1978.

Audiovisual Materials

Are You There God? It's Me, Margaret. Old Greenwich, Conn.: Listening Library, 1985. Audiocassette and book.

Are You There God? It's Me, Margaret. Old Greenwich, Conn.: Listening Library, 1988. 2 audiocassettes.

Blubber. Old Greenwich Conn.: Listening Library, 1983. Audiocassette, book, and teacher's guide.

Deenie. Old Greenwich, Conn.: Listening Library, n.d. Audiocassette, book, and teacher's guide.

Forever. New York: CBS, distributed by EMI, 1978. Videorecording.

Freckle Juice. Old Greenwich, Conn.: Listening Library, 1982. Audiocassette, book, and teacher's guide.

Iggie's House. Boston: G. K. Hall, 1986. 2 audiocassettes.

It's Not the End of the World. Old Greenwich, Conn.: Listening Library, 1985. Audiocassette and book.

The One in the Middle Is the Green Kangaroo. Old Greenwich, Conn.: Listening Library, 1983. Audiocassette, book, and teacher's guide.

Otherwise Known as Sheila the Great. Pasadena, Calif.: Barr Films, 1988. 16mm film and videorecording.

The Pain and the Great One. Old Greenwich, Conn.: Listening Library, 1986. Audiocassette and book.

Wifey. Boston: G. K. Hall, 1980. 8 audiocassettes.

Other

The Judy Blume Diary: The Place to Put Your Own Feelings.
New York: Dell, 1986.
Judy Blume Memory Book. New York: Dell, 1988.
Letters to Judy: What Your Kids Wish They Could Tell You.
New York: Putnam's, 1986; Pocket, 1987.
"1975 Sequoyah Award Acceptance Speech." *Oklahoma Librarian,* October 1975, 6–7.
"Tales of a Mother/Confessor." *Newsweek Special Issue,*
June 1990, 18–20.

SECONDARY WORKS

Books, Pamphlets, and Parts of Books

Bataglia, Frank. "If We Can't Trust: The Pertinence of Judy Blume's *Forever,"* In *Celebrating Censored Books,* edited by Nicholas J. Karolides and Lee Burress. Racine: Wisconsin Council of Teachers of English, 1985.
Broderick, Dorothy M. "Censorship: A Family Affair?" In *Young Adult Literature: Background and Criticism,* edited by Millicent Lenz and Ramona Mahood, 465–75. Chicago: American Library Association, 1980.
Commire, Anne, ed. *Something about the Author,* vol. 31. Detroit: Gale, 1983.
Donelson, Kenneth L., and Nilsen, Alleen Pace. *Literature for Today's Young Adults.* Glenview, Ill.: Scott, Foresman, 1985.
Egoff, Sheila. "The Problem Novel." In *Only Connect: Readings on Children's Literature,* edited by Sheila Egoff, G. T. Stubbs, and L. F. Ashley, 356–69. New York: Oxford University Press, 1980.
Gleasnor, Diana. *Breakthrough: Women in Writing.* New York: Walker, 1980.

Naylor, Alice Phoebe, and Wintercorn, Carol. *American Writers for Children since 1960: Fiction,* vol. 52, edited by Glenn E. Estes, 30–38. Detroit: Gale, 1986.

Rees, David. "Not Even for a One Night Stand: Judy Blume." In *The Marble in the Water: Essays on Contemporary Writers of Fiction for Children and Young Adults,* 173–84. Boston: Horn Book, 1980.

Stine, Jean C., ed. *Contemporary Literary Criticism,* vol. 30. Detroit: Gale, 1984.

Wintle, Justin, and Fisher, Emma. *The Pied Pipers.* London: Paddington, 1974.

Articles

Coburn, Randy Sue. "The Big Deal about Blume." *Washington Post Magazine,* 16 June 1985, 20.

Decter, Naomi. "Judy Blume's Children." *Commentary,* March 1980, 65–67.

Dillin, Gay Andrews. "Judy Blume: Children's Author in a Grown-Up Controversy." *Christian Science Monitor,* 29 December 1981, B4.

Donelson, Ken. "Almost 13 Years of Book Protests . . . Now What?" *School Library Journal,* March 1985, 93–98.

Eaglen, Audrey. "Answers from Blume Country: An Interview with Judy Blume." *Top of the News,* Spring 1978, 233–43.

Francke, Linda B., and Whitman, Lisa, "Growing Up with Judy." *Newsweek,* 9 October 1978, 99.

Gallo, Don. "What Should Teachers Know about YA Lit for 2004?" *English Journal,* November 1984, 31–34.

Goldberger, Judith M. "Judy Blume: Target of the Censor." *Newsletter on Intellectual Freedom,* May 1981, 57.

Gough, John. "Reconsidering Judy Blume's Young Adult Novel *Forever.*" *Use of English,* Spring 1985, 29–36.

Hamilton, Lynne. "Blume's Adolescents: Coming of Age in Limbo." *Signal,* May 1983, 88–96.

Higgins, Judith, and Kellman, Amy. "I Like Judy Blume. It's Like She Knows Me." *Teacher,* January 1979, 72–74.

Hinton-Braaten, Kathleen. "Writing for Kids Without Kidding Around." *Christian Science Monitor,* 14 May 1979, B10.

Jackson, Richard W. "Books That Blume: An Appreciation." *Elementary English,* September 1974, 779–83.

McNulty, Faith. "Children's Books for Christmas." *New Yorker,* 5 December 1983, 191–95.

Maynard, Joyce. "Coming of Age with Judy Blume." *New York Times Magazine,* 3 December 1978, 80.

Nemy, Enid. "It's Judy Blume, New Yorker." *New York Times.* 3 October 1982, 42N.

"Old Values Surface in Blume Country." *Interracial Books for Children Bulletin* 7 (1976):8–10.

Power, Jane. "Meet Judy Blume; Kid's-Eye View Draws Students . . . and Censors." *NEA Today,* October 1984, 10.

Raymond, Allen. "Judy Blume Tells It Like It Is . . . and That's Why Kids Love Her." *Early Years,* May 1984, 22–25.

Reed, J. D. "Packaging the Facts of Life." *Time,* 23 August 1982, 65.

Saunders, Paula C. "Judy Blume as Herself." *Writer's Digest,* February 1979, 18–24.

Shapiro, Jon, and Snyder, Geraldine. "Et Tu, Judy Blume: Are the Books Girls Choose to Read Sexist?" *Reading Horizons,* Summer 1982, 242–45.

Siegal, R. A. "Are You There, God? It's Me, Me, Me." *Lion and the Unicorn,* Fall 1978, 72–77.

Stanek, Lou Willett. "Just Listening: Interviews with Six Adolescent Novelists." *Arizona English Bulletin,* April 1976, 23–38.

Waddey, Lucy E. "Cinderella and the Pigman: Why Kids Read Blume and Zindel Novels." *ALAN Review,* Winter 1983, 6–9.

Films and Videorecordings

Censorship or Selection: Choosing Books for Public Schools. New York: Media & Society Seminars, 1983. Videorecording.

Children's Author—Judy Blume. 16mm, 17 min. 1980. Chicago: Films, Inc.

Profiles in Literature: Judy Blume. Philadelphia: Temple University, Department of Educational Media, 1974. Videorecording.

Book Reviews

Are You There God? It's Me, Margaret.

Booklist, 15 January 1971, 418.

Broderick, Dorothy. *New York Times Book Review,* 8 November 1970, 14.

Daane, Jeanette. *School Library Journal,* December 1970, 42.

Evans, Ann. "Blood and Tears." *Times Literary Supplement,* 7 April 1978, 383.

Hall, Ann E. "Contemporary Realism in American Children's Books." *Choice,* November 1977, 1177.

Kirkus Reviews, 1 October 1970, 1093.

Publishers Weekly, 11 January 1971, 62–63.

Sutherland, Zena. *Bulletin of the Center for Children's Books,* February 1971, 87.

Top of the News, April 1971, 305.

Blubber

Abramson, Jane. *School Library Journal,* November 1974, 54.

Booklist, 1 January 1975, 459–60.

Junior Bookshelf, August 1980, 185.

Kirkus Reviews, 1 October 1974, 1059.

Publishers Weekly, 25 November 1974, 45.

Roedder, Kathleen. *Childhood Education,* April 1975, 325.
Sachs, Marilyn. *New York Times Book Review,* 3 November 1974, 42.
Sutherland, Zena. *Bulletin of the Center for Children's Books,* May 1975, 142.
Teacher, March 1975, 112.

Deenie
Blatchford, Roy. "Down among the Hamburger Heavens," *Times Educational Supplement,* 21 November 1980, 31.
Booklist, 15 December 1973, 444.
Book World, 27 January 1974, 6.
Commonweal, 23 November 1973, 215.
Hall, Elizabeth. *Psychology Today,* September 1974, 132.
Harris, Karen. *School Media Quarterly,* Fall 1979, 27.
Junior Bookshelf, June 1981, 119.
Kellman, Amy. *Teacher,* January 1974, 112.
Kirkus Reviews, 1 September 1973, 965.
Publishers Weekly, 8 October 1973, 97.
Schroeder, Melinda. *School Library Journal,* May 1974, 53.
Sutherland, Zena. *Bulletin of the Center for Children's Books,* April 1974, 123.
Viorst, Judith. *New York Times Book Review,* 4 November 1973, 46.

Forever
Booklist, 15 October 1975, 291.
Calderone, Mary S., M.D., *Siecus Report,* May 1977, 9.
Junior Bookshelf, February 1977, 49.
Kirkus Reviews, 1 October 1975, 1136.
Minudri, Regina. *School Library Journal,* November 1975, 95.
New York Times Book Review, 28 December 1975, 20.
Nimmo, Dorothy. *School Librarian,* December 1976, 335.
Publishers Weekly, 18 August 1975, 63.
Redman, Anne. "Stay Hungry." *New Statesman,* 5 November 1976, 644.

Sutherland, Zena. *Bulletin of the Center for Children's Books,* March 1976, 106.
Times Literary Supplement, 1 October 1976, 1238.
Top of the News, Fall 1980, 57.

It's Not the End of the World
Booklist, 1 October 1972, 147.
Burns, Mary M. *Horn Book,* October 1972, 466.
Conner, John W. *English Journal,* September 1972, 936.
Elementary English, March 1973, 477.
Instructor, November 1972, 125.
Kellman, Amy. *Teacher,* May 1973, 73.
Kirkus Reviews, 14 April 1972, 3451.
School Library Journal, October 1972, 109.
Scott, Lael. *New York Times Book Review,* 3 September 1972, 8.
Sutherland, Zena. *Bulletin of the Center for Children's Books,* October 1972, 23.

Just As Long As We're Together
Booklist, August 1987, 1741.
Bradburn, Frances. *Wilson Library Bulletin,* October 1987, 61.
Humphreys, Josephine. *New York Times Book Review,* 8 November 1987, 33.
Thomas, Jane Resh. *Star Tribune,* 18 October 1987, 8Gx.

Letters to Judy
Geras, Adele. *New Statesman,* 24 October 1986, 28.
Winship, Elizabeth. *New York Times Book Review,* 8 June 1986, 12.

Otherwise Known as Sheila the Great
Booklist, 15 November 1972, 298.
Kirkus Reviews, 1 September 1972, 1025.
Library Journal, 15 May 1973, 1679.
Publishers Weekly, 14 August 1972, 46.

Smart Women
Bosworth, Patricia. *Working Woman,* March 1984, 178.
Dermansky, Ann. *New Directions for Women.* March 1984, 16.
Francke, Linda B. *New York Times,* 19 February 1984, 27.
O'Brien, Kate C. *Listener,* 16 August 1984, 26.
Teachout, Terry. *National Review,* 4 October 1985.

Starring Sally J. Freedman as Herself
Booklist, 1 June 1977, 1492.
Curriculum Review, August 1977, 206.
Haas, Diane. *School Library Journal,* May 1977, 59.
Junior Bookshelf, August 1983, 169.
Kirkus Reviews, 1 April 1977, 349.
Mercier, Jean. *Publishers Weekly,* 18 April 1977.
Nilsen, Alleen Pace. *English Journal,* February 1978, 101.
Whedon, Julia. "The Forties Revisited." *New York Times Book Review,* 1 May 1977, 40.

Superfudge
Heins, Ethel. *Horn Book,* October 1980, 518.
Pollack, Pamela D. *School Library Journal,* August 1980, 61.
Weeks, Brigitte. *Book World,* 9 November 1980, 12.

Tales of a Fourth Grade Nothing
Booklist, 1 July 1972, 941.
Kurtz, Nan Pavey. *School Library Journal,* May 1972, 74.
Sutherland, Zena. *Saturday Review,* 20 May 1972, 81.

Then Again, Maybe I Won't
Blatchford, Roy. *Time Educational Supplement,* 18 January 1980, 43.
Booklist, 1 February 1972, 465.
Broderick, Dorothy. *New York Times Book Review,* 16 January 1972, 8.
Higgins, Judith. *Teacher,* April 1973, 90.

Junior Bookshelf, October 1979, 276.
Kirkus Reviews, 1 November 1971, 1155.
Publishers Weekly, 13 December 1971, 42.
Sutherland, Zena. *Saturday Review,* 18 September 1971, 49.
Thrash, Sarah M. *School Library Journal,* April 1972, 142.
Top of the News, April 1972, 309.

Tiger Eyes
Abrahamson, Dick. *English Journal,* November 1981, 95.
Catholic Library World, September 1981, 91.
Clemons, Walter. *Newsweek,* 7 December 1981, 101.
Dillin, Gay Andrews. *Christian Science Monitor,* 14 December 1981, B10.
Greenlaw, M. Jean. *Journal of Reading,* March 1982, 609.
Junior Bookshelf, October 1982, 194.
Language Arts, April 1982, 371.
Pollack, Pamela D. *School Library Journal,* November 1981, 100.
Sutherland, Zena. *Bulletin of the Center for Children's Books,* September 1981, 5.

Wifey
Clapp, Susannah, *Times Literary Supplement,* 23 November 1979, 42.
Isaacs, Susan. *Washington Post Book World,* 8 October 1978, E5.
Publishers Weekly, 31 July 1978, 90.
Simson, Eve. *Best Sellers,* January 1979, 295.
Smothers, Joyce. *Library Journal,* 1 September 1978, 1659.

Index